the greatest love

God's Revelation to John for the World

MARILYN O. FLOWER

WESTBOW
PRESS®
A DIVISION OF THOMAS NELSON
& ZONDERVAN

WestBow Press books may be ordered through booksellers or by contacting:

WestBow Press
A Division of Thomas Nelson & Zondervan
1663 Liberty Drive
Bloomington, IN 47403
www.westbowpress.com
844-714-3454

ISBN: 978-1-6642-4255-5 (sc)
ISBN: 978-1-6642-4254-8 (hc)
ISBN: 978-1-6642-4253-1 (e)

Library of Congress Control Number: 2021916216

Print information available on the last page.

WestBow Press rev. date: 09/01/2021

In love and thanksgiving for all who hear,
endure (patiently and faithfully), stay awake,
and are ready for Christ's return.

CONTENTS

Section VIII: Heaven Bound—The Faithful Hear

Appendices

PREFACE

The Greatest Love is a call to prayerfully consider what the seven letters to the seven churches in Revelation are saying. Jesus directed the apostle John, through an angel and visions, to write and send these letters to churches in Asia Minor around 95/96 AD. Revelation, the last book in the Bible, is Jesus's urgent plea to its readers to be true to God through Him. These letters reveal early Christian beliefs that are applicable in every day. Concordant Bible passages help readers understand Revelation and know God.

Although Revelation, a book of prophecy, describes how the world will end, it is not easily understood. It continues to be debated, because people categorize events differently: literal, symbolic, or some combination of the two. All of Revelation cannot be taken literally or metaphorically, yet how readers view its chronology often determines their interpretation. Have all events happened? Are they happening now? Will they happen in the future? Conflicts arise when one group professes to have the answers and dismisses differing opinions. I believe that much of Revelation will happen in the future. Jesus's second coming may be a future event, but His kingdom is also present on earth through the Holy Spirit, who indwells those who serve God.

Even though I was born into the Christian faith and have drawn closer to God throughout my life, I believe that living encompasses more than family life, working, enjoying leisure time, and being happy. How and for whom we live makes the ultimate difference. Challenging and painful circumstances propelled me to depend more on my relationship with God and less on relating with people.

After I retired from a teaching career, I embarked on theological studies; as a result, my respect for the Bible grew, which revealed more of God and subsequently solidified my faith.

Living always involves learning. Even those who do not appreciate reading absorb information from others and from the media. Information taken in and believed becomes integral to who we are because our lives mirror our beliefs. The adage "garbage in, garbage out" is more pertinent to what we take into our minds than to what we take into our digestive systems; the nourishment that we provide our souls impacts our eternal well-being more than food feeds our bodies.

When I attended school, and taught, education encompassed more critical and creative thinking than it does today. Students were encouraged to critically evaluate everything; contrary views and counter arguments were important to understanding. Education has, however, evolved into a regurgitation of what academia and political powers deem to be true and important. Learning involves knowing facts, but understanding is paramount to exploring complex concepts such as the meaning of life. How people spend their free time reflects their beliefs. Faith in God is of far greater consequence than education, vocational training, or following a lofty goal.

One cannot read and study any portion of the Bible without discovering the battle of good against evil. Jesus came to earth to reveal God, who is perfect goodness, and expose the things of the world opposed to His virtue and righteousness. The Bible is the most important book—ever. It is the Christian's blueprint for living. The book of Revelation provides personal warnings, answers, and blessings. Jesus purposefully gave these words and visions to John to be recorded so that everyone could hear, know, and understand God's love for them, motivating them to put God first. Revelation is about death, destruction, and the final judgment of all people before Jesus heralds a new beginning. Its visions, shrouded in mystery and intrigue, and its letters reveal what it means to have faith in Jesus. The Revelation letters motivate us to want to be with God, in His will, and love as He does, but no one knows how the events portrayed in it will unfold. They incite many readers to want to know and seek the truth so that they are prepared for eternity. Jesus knows those who believe in Him, as not all who call themselves Christians follow Him. Some interpret Revelation's seven churches as historical church eras, others as different denominations, but regardless of the interpretation, Revelation is always relevant.

The words "Greater love has no one than this, that someone lay down his life for his friends" (John 15:13) may be shortened to *no greater love*. There is no greater love than the sacrificial love of Jesus, who died so that those who trust in Him might live eternally. Christians are reborn to live and love differently and know the greatest *love* that any human being can ever know. The three *t*'s in "the greatest love" remind me of Jesus and the two thieves that were crucified on either side of Him on Calvary (Luke 23:39–43). One thief was penitent, the other was not—and that made the ultimate difference. One knew God's love before he died, and heaven is his. The other never knew the greatest love that there is.

God's love turns hurt into good for those who love Him, as He did for Joseph, who was betrayed into slavery in Egypt by his brothers. Reflecting upon the pain and suffering inflicted by others, like Joseph, Christians can say, "As for you, you meant evil against me, but God meant it for good, to bring it about that many people should be kept alive, as they are today" (Gen. 50:20). Our world may be filled with anger, bitterness, confusion, and deception, but we can know far greater love than this world offers. Jesus fills Christians' hearts with gratitude, love, and joy, so that life's trials pale in comparison to God's love for us. God offers everyone, through His Son, *the* greatest love.

A work of love, this book is a sincere attempt to reach those who need the transforming love and truth of God and His Word. God transforms and changes lives, providing what this world cannot give: authentic love, peace, and joy in the ever-present faith of a glorious and eternal future. Obeying God is not a hardship when faith is genuine, even though resisting temptation is a constant struggle for even the most grounded Christian. Christians support each other by connecting in person and via technology in the power of the Holy Spirit. Bible study, prayer, and worship are paramount to their relationships with God in Christ.

This work would not have been completed without the encouragement of family, friends, and the tireless efforts of gifted editor, Iona Bulgin. Nearing its completion, my brother-in-law, Ken Butt, graciously assisted with the technological requirements for the pictures and helped me generate two maps that are much better than my sketches were. Throughout the prolonged editing process, I came to better understand and more deeply appreciate the human condition and how little we have apart from God. I send bouquets of thanks to all who supported me, especially to Ken for his graphic expertise, and to Iona for her gentle nudges and unwavering faith in God. Ultimately, God will judge and reward us.

My prayer for everyone who picks up this book is that it will motivate them to read and re-read, think and re-think, study and re-study at least chapters 2 and 3 of Revelation. By diligently seeking God, in fervent prayer and reflective Bible study, you may be forever changed and loved like you never knew was possible. Only God provides everything that everyone craves and needs. He alone makes life worth living.

> The steadfast love of the Lord never ceases; his mercies never come to an end; they are new every morning; great is your faithfulness. "The LORD is my portion," says my soul, "therefore I will hope in him." (Lam. 3:22–24)

Section I

There Is Far Greater Love

Then God said, "Let us make man in our image, after our likeness. And let them have dominion over the fish of the sea and over the birds of the heavens and over the livestock and over all the earth and over every creeping thing that creeps on the earth."

> So God created man in his own image,
> in the image of God he created him;
> male and female he created them. (Gen. 1:26–27)

Fourth-century BC ruins of the temple to Apollo, with the
seat of the Oracle of Delphi (above), and the Athenian
Treasury House (below), Delphi, Greece.

CHAPTER 1
A Word of Truth in Love

In Genesis, God gave human beings dominion over every living creature beginning with His charge to them to care for themselves in all aspects of their earthly and eternal well-being. Despite much emphasis on "personal" truth today, few people seem to recognize or appreciate God's absolute truth. Christians are taught to speak God's truth in love, even when it is unpopular, as life is precious and time is fleeting.

Our day is progressively becoming more anti-God and more pagan. Paganism, the belief in many gods, has been present in every age, as has the occult, including alchemy, astrology, divination, and magic. From antiquity, atheism has also existed. Atheists may be called agnostics, doubters, or skeptics. Some people believe that all religions are true, with many ways to God. Others say that faith is not important, as everyone goes to heaven when they die; yet others insist that death is the end.

Most Gentiles (non-Jews) were pagan at the time of Jesus's birth and for some years after His death. They believed that worshipping many gods brought safety and favor through their mystical powers. Ancient temple ruins in Asia and Europe are a reminder of the popularity of numerous Greek and Roman gods. Well-known temple priestesses or oracles, speaking for the gods, were thought to foretell the future. From the sixth century BC to the fourth century AD, the Oracle of Delphi, priestess to the Greek god Apollo, was the highest authority in the vicinity of the seven churches of Revelation, and her influence permeated the Hellenistic world.[1]

Western European and North American cultures are based on the Christian values introduced into a Jewish Greco-Roman civilization. Most Jews at the time of Jesus's birth were poor, hard-working, and marginalized. God sent His Son to be their Messiah, but He also came for the whole world. Many Jews and Christians enjoyed relatively trouble-free lives when they capitulated to the rulers and pagan beliefs of the day.

Jesus's life and His revelation to John for the seven churches help us understand the meaning and depth of God's love for His creation, and primarily for humanity.

Faith: Life and Living, Death and Dying

Our life experiences teach us that life for many is meaningless and filled with hardship. Beauty, wealth, status, and fame do not matter in the end. Faith in Jesus is the best way to live and die. God gives everyone the opportunity to find and choose Him and the free will to make that choice.

The more we advance educationally and economically, the more we realize how much is unexplainable. We think of a universe ordered beyond our best ability to understand or describe. The more it is studied, the greater is our amazement at its intricacies and orderly beauty.[2] Many conclude that it could not have happened by accident.

---

[1] "Oracle," accessed August 29, 2020, https://en.wikipedia.org/wiki/Oracle. King Croesus (of Sardis), who began testing oracles in 560 BC, believed that the Oracle of Delphi gave the most-accurate prophecies. He consulted her before he attacked Persia. It is believed that Socrates (d. 399 BC) dedicated his life to finding the truth, after the Oracle of Delphi proclaimed that there was no man wiser than he was.

[2] Episode 4 of the 2020 Netflix series *Connections—The Hidden Science of Everything* is about the irregular curve of frequency distribution of first digits known as Benford's or Newcomb-Benford Law. It describes numerical bias across various data sets. Physicist Frank Benford published "The Law of Anomalous Numbers" in *The Proceedings of American Philosophical Society* 72 (1938): 551–572. The

Humanity stands at the apex of the scientific classification of the animal kingdom. While differences between humans and other mammals are hotly debated, Christians affirm that God created all life but that only humans were created in His image. God created male and female to procreate, love one another, and care for His creation.

Faith in the God of the Bible is based on belief in Jesus as Messiah. Christians struggle to know and obey God by understanding and following the Bible, as millions have done since Jesus's death, and as the Israelites did using their scripture (the Christian Old Testament) before them. The Bible, the most-read book in the world, is the only true source of God. It informs what Christians believe and how they live, teaching accountability to God first, then government, others, and self. Not everyone is aware of God, but this does not mean that He does not exist, that the Bible is not His Word, or that anyone will escape being accountable to Him. The Bible teaches how God desires a relationship with everyone. It is replete with stories of creation, love and hate, heroes and heroines, Jesus's life and death, the beginning of His body—the church—and culminates with the book of Revelation. Those who have faith in God fear little; they know that God knows the beginning and the end and is omnipresent and sovereign.

Science teaches that humanity evolved over millions of years, yet, according to the Jewish calendar, God's record began less than six thousand years ago. The two are irreconcilable. Science has no universally accepted explanation of how life began, whereas the first book of the Old Testament, Genesis, describes its creation.

Many people are concerned about the future, especially if, when, and how life will end. Christians trust the Bible to have order and meaning, like the universe that God created, which is why some try

---

algorithm had been previously published in 1881 in the *American Journal of Mathematics* by astronomer-mathematician Simon Newcomb. This law shows how series that are expected to be random are in fact skewed but organized. It has proven useful in statistics, probability, and even fraud detection.

so hard to understand Revelation. But God discloses in His time, which is difficult for those who want to know immediately.

Revelation describes how Jesus ministers to the broken-hearted, the persecuted, the disillusioned, the hurting, and all who call to Him. His letters to the seven churches speak God's wisdom about life and death to all who will hear it. Jesus soothes their pain and carries them through trials by reassuring them that the Holy Spirit is their comfort. Through relationship with God, all people can experience how Jesus makes the eternal difference in their earthly living, to their souls, and at death. Drawn to spiritual, rather than to worldly, thinking, Christians desire godly truth, which piques their curiosity to know God even more.

Curiosity, Truth, and the Best News

News reports and social media embellish the truth in order to raise ratings and entice the masses to listen, watch, and read controversial material. "No media coverage is bad media coverage" is true for those who are biased in reporting, as they manipulate people, events, and facts. Truth may get little attention—except to be covered up—as many have appetites only for scandal, tragedy, and the bizarre. As fewer people actually do seek the truth, more items tickling the ears of those in control find their way into print and on radio, television, and the internet.

In what once were predominantly Christian countries, God's truth is considered boring and goes unreported. Everyone needs God, but, more and more, those who have their physical needs met have little use for God. Jesus is not good news to the affluent or to those who lobby for influential special interest groups. Conversely, Christians, anchored in God's truth, want to pass the good news to others as Jesus directed them to do.

Many question life and its purpose in a world where it seems that no one can be assured of hearing or even wanting the truth.[3] More and more people refuse to listen to or watch the news. They ask hard questions but rarely get answers. They seek the truth, as they are tired of hypocrisy in their communities, homes, and places of worship.

Status-quo opposers have always existed. Jesus Himself was a nonconformist who probed the thinking of the priests of His day: the Pharisees and the Sadducees, who often hid the truth and abused their authority. Jesus spoke to them of their errors, but He did it out of, and with, love. He has a vital message about the eternal security of every person—not only for those who follow Him. Jesus is the best news for any day.

Sometimes news stations broadcast inspirational stories. In January 2018, Oprah Winfrey's speech, after she received a Golden Globe lifetime achievement award, went viral. Cries for her to run for the US presidency were heard worldwide. In her speech, Oprah referred to "the insatiable dedication to uncovering the absolute truth," before she talked about personal truth.[4] What absolute truth was Oprah talking about? Neither your truth nor my truth may be true. Anything can only ever be known when it is compared to a standard. All human standards are flawed because we are flawed.

Some Christians learn about the complexity of life as they struggle to make the right choices, often counter to their human nature and to the dismay of family and friends. Jesus helps people to understand how God is the source of all truth and love. Many people ultimately

---

[3] Information is passed on as soon as it happens. Unfortunately, the "truth," even that which is purported to have been videotaped "live," may be tampered with and distorted. Deep fake videos are becoming more difficult to detect. Splicing video and audio feeds and giving half statements add to misperceptions. There are usually so many different forms and copies of the same events, however, that eventually, as lies are dispelled the truth may come out, after damage has been done, but those responsible may never be held accountable. Some question media's ethics and boundaries. Some are interested in fact-checking and presenting the truth, but too often tangly webs of lies and deception create even more confusion.

[4] Giovanni Russonello, "Read Oprah Winfrey's Golden Globes Speech," *New York Times,* January 7, 2018, accessed February 18, 2020, https://www.nytimes.com/2018/01/07/movies/oprah-winfrey-golden-globes-speech-transcript.html.

come to follow God and His truth because desperation led them to search for meaning and hope. Christians from all denominations can befriend one another, stand together, and pray for each other under the headship of Jesus Christ. Bound by the Holy Spirit and standing on God's Word, they have clarity in a world riddled with double-talk and double standards. God's truth is perfectly clear. He creates no confusion (1 Cor. 14:33); He does not obfuscate or prevaricate, as the world does. When curious minds honestly want to know the truth, they seek and find God.

Those who seek truth and believe in God through Jesus are victorious in Him. According to Revelation, when Jesus returns for His church, only the faithful will be part of it. People must get their priorities right. By seeking God, His Kingdom, and His righteousness, their eternal well-being is assured (Matt. 6:33). With the Bible as their guide, Christians have the best news to grow them in all love and truth.[5]

If we seek the things of the world, we become more like it. If we seek God, His perfect love, and His truth, we become more like Him. The Bible illustrates how God calls people to know and love Him and what He loves. Non-Christians are wise to investigate the Bible's stories; they will help them know God and understand how He rejoices in and loves people, their wholesome creativity, and their curiosity.

Jigsaw Puzzles

Contrary to the 1970 bestseller *The Late, Great Planet Earth* by Hal Lindsey and Carole C. Carlson, the Bible cannot be easily compared to a jigsaw puzzle. Like God Himself, the Bible is holy and sacred. It is the inspired and true Word of God.

Jigsaw puzzles can be challenging. It is possible to spend hours with the wrong piece in the wrong place. Light, darkness, and shadows add to the puzzle's intrigue and level of difficulty.

---

[5] One popular Christian song based on this passage is "Seek Ye First," written by Karen Lafferty in 1971. What we listen to impacts who we are. Listening to the words of the Bible either being read or sung is a valuable means of learning it.

Although eventually most puzzles are completed, no person will ever fully understand God or the Bible's simple yet extraordinarily complex message. Christians' love for God impassions them to want to know God and His Word better. Empowered by the Holy Spirit, their understanding of the Bible increases as they read it.

"At Jesus' Feet," by Nathan Greene.

> But the Lord answered her, "Martha, Martha, you are anxious and troubled about many things, but one thing is necessary. Mary has chosen the good portion, which will not be taken away from her." (Luke 10:41–42)

Although working on an intricate jigsaw puzzle may be frustrating, with persistence its completion brings satisfaction. When people persevere in understanding God's Word, they are blessed spiritually. Understanding the things of God has less to do with human effort—it is the Holy Spirit's working on a contrite heart—and more to do with the condition of the heart toward God.

Bible reading and study is holy work. No person can ever completely understand the Bible, just as they can never completely know God, but faithful people seek God through His Word to know Him better. The faithful Christian never stops trying. Like Mary, who was chastised by her sister, Martha, for not helping in the kitchen, those working to comprehend the Bible are rewarded by the One whom they seek to understand and serve, who reveals what is best for them at the appropriate time. Jesus wants us to persist in knowing God through the Bible.

You Must Not Do That!

Every word of the Bible is true and trustworthy. People are accurately represented, with some of their worst flaws highlighted. The Bible reveals that Jesus alone did not sin.

We sometimes think that biblical characters, writers, theologians, and first-century Christians were close to sinless. Not so. Few lived godly lives and only one had a heart like God's. That was David. Although the biblical writers wrote under God's authority and in the power of the Holy Spirit, God ensured that their flaws were recorded for our benefit. God used and continues to use weak and broken people to deliver His truth.

Consider John. Just after the fourth blessing in Revelation 19:9,

John fell at the angel's feet to worship him, but he was quickly admonished: "'You must not do that! I am a fellow servant with you and your brothers who hold to the testimony of Jesus. Worship God.' For the testimony of Jesus is the spirit of prophecy" (Rev. 19:10). Although the angel warned John not to worship anyone but God, John erred a second time:

> I, John, am the one who heard and saw these things. And when I heard and saw them, I fell down to worship at the feet of the angel who showed them to me, but he said to me, "You must not do that! I am a fellow servant with you and your brothers the prophets, and with those who keep the words of this book. Worship God." (Rev. 22:8–9)

As he watched the vision of the river of life and the angel's revelation of Jesus's return, just after the sixth blessing, John forgot the angel's chastisement (Rev. 19:10) and bent again to worship the angel.

John was likely familiar with the letters that Paul had written to the early church. Paul had warned Christians in Colossae against worshipping angels; some had been tempted to fall away from orthodoxy in this way (Col. 2:18). John had forgotten this admonition twice (even more, if he knew of Paul's letter to Colossae) but included his own sin in the book of Revelation. John's record of his sin has encouraged many throughout the centuries and should encourage readers today.

If one of the greatest apostles did sin, it is easy for us to sin. We may not believe that worshipping angels is as grievous as worshipping idols, icons, or graven images, but all sin is against God, must be repented of, and forgiven. Passages like this show that even godly people sin. Peter is another apostle who, after showing his fallen nature, greatly blessed the church. Although he had denied Jesus three times, he went on to powerfully spread the good news of Jesus Christ. Peter's two epistles encourage those enduring persecution for their faith: they remind Christians to live holy and godly lives, speak of God's grace, and warn the church against false teachers and heresy.

Because Peter believed in Jesus as God and was transformed, God used him mightily. Peter did not place himself on a pedestal but saw himself as a mere man with human needs and ways.[6] He was convicted by Jesus to testify to His love and sacrifice for all people.

Everything in the Bible has purpose. It provides a wealth of truth to edify and encourage everyone to live in, but not become part of, the world, as John and Peter learned to do through Jesus. The Holy Spirit ensured that nothing of God's Word was withheld just to make anyone look good. But the Bible must be read with faith.

Living in the World While Not Being of It

The preposition *in* means that something is present, accessible, or available. If people are in the world, they are alive. There is no need to know anything about the world in order to understand the people. We are in the world until we die; then we are no longer in it. *Of*, another preposition, means being part of something larger. Both parts of the "living in the world while not being of the world" concept must be understood.

Jesus lived *in* the world, but He was never *of* the world. In John 8:23, He said, "You are from below; I am from above. You are of this world; I am not of this world." He was from above, meaning heaven. Those to whom He spoke were from the natural world; they were of the world, not merely living in it. Jesus is fully man and fully God. He had the human potential to sin when He lived on the earth, but He did not sin. It is impossible for anyone to fully understand these mysteries. Jesus was tempted in His humanity, but by not yielding to these temptations, He won humanity's spiritual battle for them, thus epitomizing the difference between living in the world and not

---

[6] The first four books of the New Testament, called the gospels, record Jesus's healing Peter's mother-in-law at their home in Capernaum (Matt. 8:14–15; Mark 1:29–31; Luke 4:38–39). The early church fathers Clement and Eusebius believed that Paul too was married. Paul asked, "Do we not have the right to take along a believing wife, as do the other apostles and the brothers of the Lord and Cephas?" (1 Cor. 9:5); this tells us that at least some of the apostles and Jesus's brothers were married.

being of it. Jesus was not of the world, but the devil is of the world. Christians are called to not be of the world.

The world is where we live. To say that people are of the world means that they are worldly or of the same spiritual essence as all the people of the world: Christians and non-Christians. Christians live in the world, but they are called not to be *of* it. If they were *of* the world, they would go along with all that the world believes and values and be under the devil's rule. Redeemed by Jesus's blood, Christians must struggle to live righteous and sober lives, repent of sin, and live differently from how the world lives and how the devil wants them to live.

John wrote of the difference between being *in* the world and being *of* the world, particularly in John 15:18–25 and 17:11–17. In John 15:19, John records Jesus as saying, "If you were of the world, the world would love you as its own; but because you are not of the world, but I chose you out of the world, therefore the world hates you." Such passages are difficult for Christians to understand but with study and careful reflection these verses help them discern how they must live. Some Christians look with concern at other "Christians" who are well accepted by the world, especially because Jesus preached that Christians living differently from the world would be hated as He is hated. Christians are assured of dying only once. After this comes judgment, and heaven for those known by Christ. Jesus commissions Christians to pass on their faith and biblical knowledge to others, especially to their children.

Parents are responsible for raising their children well, especially spiritually. Adequate childcare worldwide includes physical, emotional, social, and mental support, but spiritual care, which is more important, is rarely mentioned. Ready access to material resources and money does not ensure a healthy, safe environment for anyone. Christians know how imperative it is that they teach their children and grandchildren about God and His awesome love for them.

The Bible says that Christians are to love God with all their heart, mind, body, and strength. They are to put God first, but statistics show that few do. The world's richest nations put their faith in economics, education, science, and political might. One Barna research study showed that in some cases the strongest Christians "are even more pragmatic and career-focused than non-Christians. Moral and spiritual development are important but not the best reason to pursue a college education."[7] According to this study, most Christian youth attending university rank faith after academics. Parents desire the best education for their children, but Christian parents do not want their children's education to cost them their faith. When Christians consider faith less important than financial security and worldly success, it follows that we cannot expect to live in a spiritually healthier world than the one we presently inhabit.

In Western civilization, Christian values existed alongside scientific thinking and advanced reasoning. Christians worked with non-Christians to improve the standard of living through founding Christian hospitals, schools, and universities. In recent decades, as Christianity has drastically declined in many affluent nations, horrendous incidents of abuse and scandal have been exposed—as they should. Centuries-old evils such as the exploitation of children and scientific racism, responsible for untold hatred, genocide, eugenics, and human zoos, often organized and led by "Christians," may have been covered up, but God always knew. Such deplorable sin continues to cast a long shadow over the church, but it must not be allowed to taint God's goodness and love. Complete honesty is the only Christian option. Lies and cover-ups must be revealed, repented of, and never repeated.

Christians lovingly fight that which is anti-God and anti-Christ because they love God first, and then they love all people. They know that God's love of people surpasses theirs. They see how faith in God often decreases as material wealth and power grow, because God, unlike the world, disapproves of selfish, sinful lifestyles. Many are lulled into silence out of fear for their own safety. Because truth is

---

[7] "Do Christian Students Want Spiritual Growth from College?," accessed September 5, 2018, www.barna.com/research/spiritual-growth-college/?utm_source=Barna+Update.

not taught, either in the public square or in many churches, more and more non-Christians capitulate to liberal agendas. Many Christians, too, feel that it is unsafe to stand against popular opinion, because the world ridicules belief in a God who does not conform to cultural norms.

In the World Until We Are No Longer

God created humankind to relate personally with each other in community, as He does with Jesus and the Holy Spirit. But we are created to relate to God first. The death of the body is the great equalizer. Gender, race, color, age, wealth, power, status, title, and education level are unimportant. Nothing matters but faith in God.

Jesus came to earth to heal us spiritually. Physical healing was not His priority, but often before He could speak of spiritual matters, He had to deal with urgent physical ones. Jesus told those following Him, "Let us go on to the next towns, that I may preach there also, for that is why I came out" (Mark 1:38). Jesus's mission was to save souls. When He returns, He will judge. In order to love other people and spread the good news of Jesus Christ to them, Christians often provide basic material needs in tandem with spreading the gospel.

The trials and pains of this life are all temporary. The Bible, in contrast, teaches that heaven and hell are real and that separation from God results in real eternal pain. For Christians, this world is the worst hell that they will ever experience; for non-Christians, this world is the best heaven that they will ever know. Christians do not want anyone to miss heaven; they know that the best is yet to come. Unrepented sin, however, is against God. It maims, kills, and results in eternal pain.

"What is life about?" "What happens when we die?" "Is there a God?" "Is Jesus God?" "Will Jesus return to earth?" "Who is God; how do I get to know Him?" and "How can I know that what I believe is true?" Some honestly asking such questions are led to read the Bible. To understand the Bible better we should know about the belief systems at the time of, and prior to, its writing, because these same systems are all alive today.

God created everything: archaeology, history, science, and government. In many nations, people are free to study and explore any academic subject they wish, but their comprehension of that material is only optimized when God is present. God detests the lies of alternate facts and fake news. He alone is the whole truth. People who seek truth do not fear questions; they want honest answers. God desires that everyone seek Him to have their deep longings for truth satisfied.

God's Invitation

> The Spirit and the Bride say, "Come." And let the one who hears say, "Come." And let the one who is thirsty come; let the one who desires take the water of life without price. (Rev. 22:17)

God invites everyone to come to Him. Jesus sent an angel to testify to John for seven churches in Asia Minor (Rev. 22:16), but the teachings in these seven letters are for all people everywhere. They transcend time. The Bible contains a host of godly invitations that illustrate the loving nature of God. Jesus's account of the woman at the well in John 4:5–42 poignantly illustrates how He knows everything about everyone, yet lovingly beckons even the worst sinners to come to Him. Jesus died so that everyone, without exception, might be saved, redeemed, forgiven, and experience eternal life.

The good news of Jesus Christ has been preached for almost two thousand years. It has been in print, not in the same form or language as we now know it, but written on scrolls, for several decades less. Revelation, the last written, was delivered to the churches in modern-day Turkey after the death of Antipas in 92 AD, possibly 95/96 AD.[8] In it, Jesus spoke openly of the churches' ties

---

[8] Antipas, bishop of Pergamum, mentioned once in the Bible (Rev. 2:13), is discussed in Chapter 5.

to the world. He pleaded with them to overcome their sin, drink of His spiritual living water, and be victorious in faith.

Reading and studying the Bible is easier, more enjoyable, and more productive when maps, historical documents, and other research materials, such as archaeological articles, books, and videos, are used. The readers' questions will often prompt further research. Bible references must be always checked, and cross checked with other versions, as Bible versions vary greatly. Godly discernment of every matter of faith and the Bible is crucial.

The following map illustrates the first-century biblical world. Christianity spread out quickly from Jerusalem after Jesus's crucifixion. Alexandria, Antioch, Byzantium (later known as Constantinople and then Istanbul), and Rome were pivotal Christian centers in the first century. Note the geographical regions of these centers and other early communities in relationship to Jerusalem, the City of Truth (Zech. 8:3 KJV). These five Christian centers are marked with a cross. The seven locations that received New Testament epistles are highlighted by an open book.

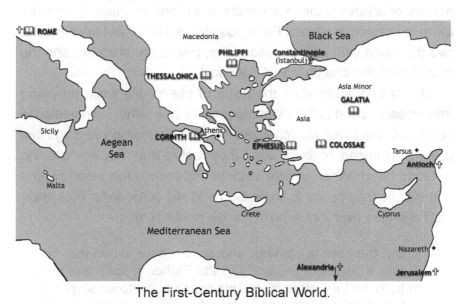

The First-Century Biblical World.

The New Testament, sometimes erroneously considered the only Christian part of the Bible, describes Jesus's life, death, ascension, and the early church, but the whole Bible is God's invitation to come to Him. Everyone who needs their thirst for the meaning of life quenched is invited by Jesus to come, listen, read, and drink of Him.

In honestly seeking God, Christians want to know Him and what He deems is right and true. Because many pretenders want to be God, it is vital that the only reliable source—the Word of God—be consulted to verify everything. Christians must begin each Bible study session in prayer, thanking God and asking Him to oversee their study so that what is learned is only of Him.

This book invites all readers to examine or re-examine their lives through seven letters sent to seven churches in the first century AD. Digesting what Jesus says to the churches and applying His messages honestly to their own lives will spur some to re-think their values and perhaps motivate them to want to know more about God and lead to further Bible study.

Understanding the history of Christianity and the church helps Christians and non-Christians better know and understand God, His ways and purposes, the Bible, and Christian beliefs. One means of studying these subjects is to look at them in smaller, more manageable pieces. For a possible aid to begin looking at the two thousand years since Jesus's life, death, resurrection, and the inception of the church, see Appendix I.

Jesus offers everyone the hope of eternal life while providing fresh meaning and purpose for the present one. What He revealed to John for those seven churches over nineteen hundred years ago can profoundly impact readers when they realize that they are listening to God's heart. When people seek to understand this small portion of the Bible they desire to know God and His purpose for their lives. God changes everyone who sincerely seeks Him.

> But the hour is coming, and is now here, when the true worshipers will worship the Father in spirit and truth, for the Father is seeking such people to worship him. God is spirit, and those who worship him must worship in spirit and truth. (John 4: 23–24)

Section II

God's Revelation

Come and hear, all you who fear God,
and I will tell what he has done for my soul.
I cried to him with my mouth,
and high praise was on my tongue.
If I had cherished iniquity in my heart,
the Lord would not have listened.
But truly God has listened;
he has attended to the voice of my prayer.
Blessed be God,
because he has not rejected my prayer
or removed his steadfast love from me! (Ps. 66:16–20)

Come to me, all you who are weary and burdened,
and I will give you rest. Take my yoke upon you and
learn from me, for I am gentle and humble in heart,
and you will find rest for your souls. For my yoke is
easy and my burden is light. (Matt. 11:28–30 NIV)

Mars Hill, Athens, Greece, stairs (above) and
the view from the hilltop (below).

CHAPTER 2
Come, Hear, and Believe

E veryone can come to know God's love through Jesus, who points to His Father in relationship with Him and the Holy Spirit. Christians learn about God through the Old and New Testaments of the Bible. Before Christ, prophets and faithful kings of the Old Testament encouraged people to hear about God. The first four books, or gospels, of the New Testament give an account of Jesus's life. The fifth book, Acts, written by the third gospel writer, Luke, reveals early church history, including the dramatic conversion of the Pharisee Saul on the road to Damascus.

Saul heard Jesus's voice, believed, and, as Paul, was ready to evangelize Jews, but God called him to reach the Gentiles.[9] About half of the New Testament was written by and/or about Paul, who warned his hearers not to "be conformed to this world, but be transformed by the renewal of your mind, that by testing you may discern what is the will of God, what is good and acceptable and perfect" (Rom. 12:2). Paul, as a Jew, knew God, but he learned, as a dedicated Jesus follower, to love God.

Among the first phrases attributed to Jesus were invitations to come and follow Him, first to the twelve apostles and then to the

---

[9] Greatly troubled by the number of idols and divination in Athens, Paul was drawn into conversation with philosophers who invited him to address the Areopagus one day after he had reasoned with some Jews in the synagogue. Paul's speech to the elite of Athens, in which he confronted their idolatry, is his fullest, most-dramatic speech recorded in the New Testament. See Acts 17:16–34.

crowds. In the first gospel, Matthew records how Jesus responded to those opposing John the Baptist's and His ministry and to those who tried to entrap Him or encouraged and threatened people to stay away from Him and His followers: Jewish leaders, scribes, and Pharisees. But Jesus told the people to come and He would relieve their burdens (Matt. 11:25–30).

Jesus's invitations were personal, going beyond following Him and believing in who He was or in the miracles that He did. They went beyond offering the hope of rest from weary, difficult lives. Jesus's invitations were to come and know God through Him. Still today, Jesus speaks through the Bible to Christians crushed under the weight of false teaching, heretical religious practice, and political and cultural oppression. Matthew's gospel was written primarily to evangelize Jews by convincing them that Jesus was their long-awaited Messiah, despite what looked like defeat at the cross but revealed that Jesus had come for the Gentiles as well.[10] God inspired Matthew to recall the words and deeds of Jesus that he had witnessed, including much scripture that contained messianic prophecies. Matthew had walked with Jesus, as crowds of people gathered to listen, and he had watched Him heal the sick. He wrote of Jewish feasts and festivals that related to their Hebrew history and encouraged fellow Jews, despite their variant beliefs, to come to faith in Jesus as he had done.

There were zealots, Pharisees, Sadducees, and other Jewish sects in the first century, but Jesus's main purpose was to lift the burdens of the Jewish masses. Jesus's knowledge of and teaching from Hebrew Scripture assured many Jews that they were following their Messiah. Other Jews watched and waited for a strong warrior-king, like David, to lead Israel again to worldly power.

Today, many who rely on worldly power detest dualities—good and evil, light and dark, peace and war, male and female, right and

---

[10] Papias, bishop of Hierapolis, in modern-day Turkey (c.60–130 AD), and Irenaeus, bishop of Lyons, in Gaul (c.175), both attributed the first gospel to Matthew Levi, a Jew, former tax collector, and disciple of Jesus. Most, if not all, of the New Testament writers were Jewish.

wrong—and resist the gospel of Jesus Christ because God's Word stands on dualisms. The Bible reassures Christians that they form Christ's body and are linked through the Bible, the Holy Spirit, and prayer. The worldwide church is also linked today via technology: it not only meets in person but, via the internet, it comes together in praise and worship to read and study the Bible, and to learn, share, and help one another "as iron sharpens iron" (Prov. 27:17).

Belief in Jesus gives all who follow Him the assurance of eternity. Many today believe that the world is getting better and more peaceful, but reality does not support this. The Bible teaches that the world will become progressively more evil and ultimately will be destroyed by fire. Jesus invites every person to come, hear, believe, be relieved of their oppression, experience true love, and be assured of heaven.

Loved Like You Have Never Been Loved

Those who diligently seek God find Him (Prov. 8:17). His love for us is unquantifiable and unexplainable. It is impossible to genuinely love anyone without first loving God because God is love. We cannot give His kind of love unless we have experienced it ourselves. We will never know God fully, but we can welcome the Holy Spirit to influence our thoughts so that we can spread love to others.

God wants us to find His will for our lives even when it involves questioning or being angry with Him, regardless of the number or severity of our sins. Genesis 32:22 to 33:11 describe Jacob's wrestling with God as he fled his father-in-law, Laban, and sought his brother, Esau. Either God Himself or His messenger forced Jacob to confront his fears, struggles, and weaknesses and to seek God's will. The event left Jacob marked forever by God. His limp, a result of his out-of-joint hip, was a constant reminder of this encounter.

Despite all that Jacob had done wrong, God loved him. After Jacob experienced God's love, as he could not before, he was restored to Esau. Able to repent, be forgiven, and love Esau as God loved them both, Jacob was a transformed man. Despite his sin, Jacob, now Israel, became the father of its twelve tribes. He was changed physically, emotionally, and spiritually. Honestly seeking God is painful. It leaves indelible marks, but its fruit is priceless to those who know God's great love.

All who diligently seek God will find Him because they love and want to be true to Him before anyone or anything else. They seek God's heart and will, because they have learned, often through pain and heartache, the futility of seeking the world and its people. While seeking God, they learn that what He allows works together for their benefit. People do need one another, but they need God more. Despite the kindnesses we can show to each other, we often do not. We also cannot make anyone part of God's family. Only Jesus can do that. One day Jesus will return and everyone will see Him, but for those who have not accepted Him, it will be too late. Compassionate people may be kind and loving to everyone, but they cannot save others or themselves.

Why are there so few Christians? Why are some of the richest, most privileged, and famous of our time perpetuating evil and/or taking their own lives? Money is not the answer. Nor is fame. Being rich and famous often creates more problems than it solves. So, what does bring contentment and peace? The Bible describes the source of contentment, peace, and genuine love: Jesus alone satisfies the human quest for love, fulfillment, and life's true meaning.

Seventeenth-century mathematician and philosopher Blaise Pascal, who forsook his earthly possessions to seek God, is credited with the idea that a God-shaped hole exists in everyone's heart that only He can fill. The following quotation, from *Pensées*, alludes to this concept. Pascal's conversion led to his ascetic life.

> What else does this craving, and this helplessness, proclaim but that there was once in man a true happiness, of which all that now remains is the empty print and trace? This he tries in vain to fill with everything around him, seeking in things that are not there the help he cannot find in those that are, though

none can help, since this infinite abyss can be filled only with an infinite and immutable object; in other words by God himself.[11]

God alone can fill this dark and unfathomable void. It is easy for Christians to know what non-Christians need, because they have it—true love: the love of God and His truth and an authentic relationship with Him. For those who do not know Jesus, the world offers temporal happiness through fleshly pleasures, worldly goals, and material possessions. Pascal discovered that there is no substance in temporal happiness, but many today have yet to realize that.

Everyone needs Jesus, but asceticism is a personal choice.

Every Eye Will See Him

Behold, he is coming with the clouds, and every eye will see him, even those who pierced him, and all the tribes of the earth will wail on account of him. Even so. Amen. "I am the Alpha and the Omega," says the Lord God, "who is and who was and who is to come, the Almighty." (Rev. 1:7–8)

John recorded all that he heard and saw. He knew that his vivid visions came from Jesus, were urgent, must be recorded, and sent immediately to the seven churches, but he likely did not fully understand them. John did not see into the future. But Jesus not only knows the future, He controls it.

When Jesus returns to earth, everyone at that time will have had an opportunity to hear the gospel and choose to come to Christ. Every eye will see Him return as He left—even those who "pierced" Him, those responsible for His death (Rev. 1:7). The specifics are unknown, but everyone who has ever lived will see Jesus and know that He is God.

---

[11] Blaise Pascal, *Pensées,* 2nd ed. (1670). *Pensées,* meaning *thoughts* in English, is his most influential theological work.

After Jesus's resurrection, Cleopas and another man met Him on the road to Emmaus, but did not know Him. They saw, but did not understand. Only after Jesus explained the importance of scripture, broke and blessed bread, and gave it to them were their eyes opened to recognize Him. Afterwards, the two told the apostles how Jesus had opened their minds to understand scripture and why He had suffered and bodily risen from the grave on the third day. Just before His ascension to heaven, Jesus blessed His disciples and told them that true repentance and forgiveness of sins must be "proclaimed in his name to all nations, beginning from Jerusalem" (Luke 24:47–48).

The gospels reveal that most of Nazareth did not believe that Jesus was the Son of God.[12] Jesus knew that He would not be believed in His hometown. Not even His brothers, two of whom later wrote New Testament letters, believed in Him until after His resurrection. Jesus said, "A prophet is not without honor, except in his hometown and among his relatives and in his own household" (Mark 6:4–5). He healed a few people there, but otherwise Jesus performed no miracles.

John knew much about eyes being enabled to *see*. His record of Jesus's healing a man born blind is followed by teaching on spiritual blindness (John 9:35–41; 12:37–40). John's spiritual sight was sharper than that of the other apostles. He knew that one with good vision but be spiritually blind, just as another who is blind can spiritually see.

Open Eyes, Ears, Minds, and Hearts

If those walking the earth with Jesus had difficulty knowing Him, we should not be surprised by how few eyes and ears are spiritually open in our day. Eyes remain shut until God opens them. Sometimes this is due to hardened hearts and closed minds. God alone knows

---

[12] See Matthew 13:54–58; Mark 6:1–6; Luke 4:16–30; and John 4:44; 6:42; 7:15; 10:39.

what lies ahead, but one day Jesus will return and everyone who ever lived will give an account of their lives to Him.

In Acts, sometimes considered a continuation of Luke's gospel, we read of the church's establishment and how Christianity spread. Life in the Roman Empire was especially difficult for Christians. They were exempt from worshipping other gods at first, as they were considered a Jewish sect. As they became visibly distinct from the Jews, their refusal to worship emperors and pagan gods brought them severe consequences.

Christians drew strength from the Hebrew Scripture from which Jesus taught, recalling, for example, the Exodus, Jewish feasts, and the Babylonian exile, when Daniel and his friends resisted the temptation to submit to those in power. Such Old Testament passages have warmed the hearts of Jewish and Gentile Christians since the first century, encouraging them to stand firm and be courageous.

The apostles had little faith in Christ while He was physically with them, but all of them, except John, were martyred for their faith after the Holy Spirit opened their spiritual eyes to understand that Jesus is Lord. Standing on God's truth, Christians "know that the Son of God has come and has given us understanding, so that we may know him who is true, and we are in him who is true, in his Son Jesus Christ. He is the true God and eternal life" (1 John 5:20). They know God through the Bible. God opens eyes, ears, minds, and hearts when He chooses. Cleopas, the apostles, and Jesus's siblings could not understand or believe until they could spiritually see and hear.

The ability to see and hear spiritually is the key to discerning what is of God. Christians love God more than their own lives or families. Their first desire is to spread God's truth and love. In the early church, the faithful lived courageously for Christ, spreading the gospel because of their spiritual discernment. Under the Holy Spirit the church flourished, even as prideful, weak, and ambitious individuals within it began to cause division, hatred, and heresy. But as churches grew in wealth, hierarchy, and prestige, some fell deeper into corruption and apostasy, just as the Israelites had.

Old and New Testament people had difficulty hearing, seeing, and believing. The Bible frequently talks about the importance of hearing and seeing.[13] Proverbs 20:12 speaks of hearing ears and seeing eyes as being created purposefully by God. Ears may hear and absorb some information due to prior knowledge and an understanding of the vocabulary, but spiritual concepts may not be fully understood. The ability to listen to or read words does not mean that the person with ears hears or understands, nor with eyes sees or knows. The hearing ear and the seeing eye mean more than merely sensory function and basic literal comprehension. They imply that hearers and see-ers also spiritually understand. Hearers and see-ers inwardly comprehend God's Word deep within their spirits.

Old Testament prophets describe how God eventually shut the eyes and ears of the Israelites because their hearts were hard and far from Him. About seven hundred years before Jesus's birth, the prophet Isaiah wrote, "They know not, nor do they discern, for he has shut their eyes, so that they cannot see, and their hearts, so that they cannot understand" (Isa. 44:18). God used Israel's hardness of heart after Christ's death to graft wild shoots into the *olive* tree.[14]

In Romans 11:1–10, written in the middle of the first century, Paul quotes Deuteronomy, Ezekiel, and Jeremiah, among others, to explain how only a few had followed Christ, the Jewish Messiah. In his third and final plea to the Israelites, Moses urged them to follow God's covenant: "But to this day the Lord has not given you a heart to understand or eyes to see or ears to hear" (Deut. 29:4). God, who knows every individual, cherishes the softened hearts turned to Him and opens their eyes and ears to see and hear Him spiritually, in His

---

[13] The Biblical references to ears and eyes, such as those in Isaiah 43:8, Matthew 13:16, and Mark 8:18, imply a deep faith and trust in God. Through the Holy Spirit, God provides these faithful hearers with a spiritual comprehension of the text that surpasses any initial or commonly held perfunctory meaning.

[14] Of the seven species that the Bible espouses as valuable to Israel—wheat, barley, figs, olives, grapes, dates, and pomegranates—the grape vine, fig tree, and olive tree have been used symbolically to refer to Israel.

time. Despite all that God had done for the Israelites, they moaned and complained and their disobedient hearts remained hard. In His appointed time, God hardens hearts and takes away any possibility of spiritual sight or hearing.

The prophets Isaiah, Jeremiah, and Ezekiel condemned Israel's disobedience. Jeremiah condemned the eyes and ears of Israel and Judah (Jer. 5:21); likewise, Ezekiel chastised Judah (Ezek. 12:2). From their beginning, the Israelites generally had a poor record of obeying God. Despite the prophets' warnings and encouragement to return to the Lord, they kept returning to their idolatrous ways. Appealing to Jewish Christians to understand their heritage as God's chosen people, but also to understand their sin, Paul describes how God would use the time of the remnant's disobedience to allow a predetermined number of Gentiles to be brought to Him (Rom. 11:11–24).[15]

Early Christians, like the Israelites, wavered from obedience to disobedience. We too can become angry and bitter when we think that God has been unjust and unloving. Jews and Gentiles alike have a selfish nature. Christians, although redeemed, still revert to sinful ways, quickly forgetting God's Word. It is easy to understand why the Bible reminds its readers repeatedly to hear and see.

For those who are ready, with hearts prepared to hear, God appeals to their senses and emotions to help them understand what He wants them to know so that they may comprehend His ways and follow His direction. In the Old Testament, God used creation and the growth of families and nations to show how He loves and draws people to Himself. He also used stories of brokenness, pain, forgiveness, redemption, faithfulness, and courage. God used Israel's history—its patriarchs, judges, prophets, and kings, and their failures and successes—to show Israel, and all the earth, why it was necessary for Jesus to come to earth as Messiah.

---

[15] To better understand Israel's place in faith and salvation, see chapters 9 to 11 of Paul's letter to the Romans and the Old Testament passages to which Paul refers. In both Old and New Testaments, the word *remnant* refers to those faithful to God. In the Old Testament, it refers to the remaining faithful Jews; in the New Testament, it refers to the remaining faithful Christians.

The New Testament uses the Old Testament to clarify truth. Jesus often used Hebrew Scripture to help His followers know who He was and why He had come. He also spoke in parables to help people understand, because many did not hear or see as Christians empowered by the Holy Spirit do. The parable of the wheat and the weeds (Matt. 13:24–30) describes how good and evil coexist in the church until Jesus comes to judge, when He will separate those who believe from those who do not. It is sometimes easier to see good when it is among evil. Christians must read and understand the Bible to know that they must not judge but be wary of their surroundings.

The New Testament follows the Hebrew way of teaching; Jesus uses concrete examples from first-century life: fishing, farming, carpentry, family, trials, and tribulations. In appealing to the senses, parables help people reflect on what is being said, and, in this way, they learn. In Matthew 13:13, Jesus explains why He uses them: "This is why I speak to them in parables, because seeing they do not see, and hearing they do not hear, nor do they understand." Similarly, Paul, drawing upon Greek life, uses games, comparing faith to running and winning a race. Through parabolic teaching and comparing life to a race, some ears hear and some eyes see and understand, thus allowing God to draw people closer.

In Matthew 24:14, after foretelling the Temple's destruction, Jesus talks about the signs before His second coming: "And this gospel of the kingdom will be proclaimed throughout the whole world as a testimony to all nations, and then the end will come." This verse assures us that everyone will have heard the gospel before Jesus returns.[16] No one should worry about when Jesus will return, for "no one knows, not even the angels in heaven, nor the Son, but only the Father" (Mark 13:32).

---

[16] Joshua Project, accessed June 5, 2021, https://joshuaproject.net. We are close to having the Bible reach every tribe and nation. Still, millions have not heard the gospel. The Bible has yet to be translated into approximately two thousand more languages.

Although the day or hour of Christ's return is unknown, some spend much time speculating how close we are to it. God commands Christians to love and know Him and His Word so that they are equipped to preach the gospel to the ends of the earth. We must use our eyes and ears to be so familiar with the Bible that instead of looking for signs of Christ's second coming, they are no surprise when they do occur.

In God's Time

God, who created time and space, is outside of it. In our inability to understand, we often attempt to put God within our chronological timeframe. God's thoughts and ways are unexplainable, His miraculous signs and wonders indescribable. We are not to look for miraculous and wondrous signs but to rejoice when they do appear. They are gifts that assure us of God's love and presence.

Reading the Bible or having it read to you is a sacred act of love. Reading it to tear it apart is sacrilege. Reading in hate cannot be met with any understanding. God assures us that His every word is precious, has purpose (Isa. 55:11), and, for softened hearts, will accomplish what God purposes it to do. Every one of God's words has power. The wise seize every opportunity to concentrate on God's powerful Word.

God's timing is impeccable. He is patient and will hold us up when we need it, support us during our trials, and wait for us to understand. With God, "a day is like a thousand years, and a thousand years are like a day. The Lord is not slow in keeping his promise, as some understand slowness. He is patient with you, not wanting anyone to perish, but everyone to come to repentance" (2 Pet. 3:8–9 NIV). In God's time, those called will see and repent.

Likewise, in God's time, Jesus will return for His church. Christians must wait patiently. We must be ready always because we do not know when Jesus will return.

> Now concerning the times and the seasons, brothers and sisters, you do not need to have anything written to you. For you yourselves know very well that the day of the Lord will come like a thief in the night. When they say, "There is peace and security," then sudden destruction will come upon them, as labor pains come upon a pregnant woman, and there will be no escape! (1 Thess. 5:1–3 NRSV)

Some Christians use every opportunity to preach the gospel, even when doing so is met with hostility. Often their lives speak the loudest, convicting others to desire God.

Sharing faith in God can be intimidating. Honesty is often not appreciated and, while one must be forthright, it is important to be loving, and non-judgmental. Despite what seems to be an urgency to pass the gospel to loved ones, it is important to be sure that what is spoken is fully God's truth and in His time. The Bible, the Christians' source of learning about God and truth, is sometimes viewed as hate literature, while the sacred texts of other religions are given respect. Too often this is the reality in countries that were founded on Christian principles, but God's will will come to pass in His time.

Ironically, one of the safest places to read and study the Bible is in prison, where some inmates come to know that "God blesses those people who depend only on Him. They belong to the kingdom of heaven" (Matt. 5:3 CEV). Inmates, at their lowest points, are often open to reading and studying the Bible, praying, and being prayed for. Those whom God calls to come to faith in prison find genuine hope of a fresh beginning. It is often those who are not incarcerated, yet who live outside of God's will for their lives, that are imprisoned by their fear of admitting that they need God.

Come Know God's Love

> But blessed are your eyes, for they see, and your
> ears, for they hear. (Matt. 13:16)

Everyone is created fully equal in God's eyes. Although we have various strengths and needs, the essence of what makes us human is our free will to choose or reject God. The intellectually challenged may sing God's praises, while the genius curses Him; a gifted scientist may worship the God who created him or her in sincerity and reverence, while a laborer takes God's name in vain, oblivious to His existence and His power.

The prophet Jeremiah documented God's desire that His chosen people answer the call to come to Him: "I will give them a heart to know that I am the LORD, and they shall be my people and I will be their God, for they shall return to me with their whole heart" (Jer. 24:7). The Old Testament documents the collective, yet vacillating, faith of the nation of Israel over generations as compared to the individual trust in Jesus of the Christians of the New Testament who represent every tribe and nation.

No one can accept Jesus as Savior and Lord in their own strength unless God gives them the desire to do so. It does not matter how moral or spiritual one is; until God calls, no one is saved. God knows every mind and heart and calls each one in His time. When He calls, it is up to each person to accept Jesus and know God's perfect love.

Relating personally with God is most important because He created us to have a relationship with Him. God gives us what He knows we need, not what we want. Getting a "need" instead of a "want" is not well accepted in an affluent, changing world that believes God changes too. Often people are not ready to know God until they come to the end of themselves and realize that they need something greater than what they want or the world offers. There is no way to know or predict when God will call, but He, who is perfect justice, knows when each heart is ready to know and love Him.

John, an expert on God's *agape* and *agapeo* love, Greek forms of the noun and verb of godly love, explains God's love. After Jesus revealed His relationship to God by teaching the first of seven *I Am* statements to the crowd following Him, the Jews who heard these statements ostracized Him because of His being Joseph and Mary's son. Similarly, today some are branded by their worldly heritage rather than their worth in God's eyes. Jesus rebuked the Jews' spiritual immaturity: "No one can come to me unless the Father who sent me draws him. And I will raise him up on the last day" (John 6:44). Clearly, these Jews were not ready to be called to salvation.

No one escapes life without hurting and being hurt. Pain often causes people to question truth, love, and life's purpose. God, the source of all love, draws people to Himself. He invites them to drink the water of life and eat the bread of heaven that only He can provide.

Jesus commanded His apostles to come and see Him and what He would do before His public ministry, and crowds of people began to follow Him. The apostles had little idea initially of what "coming and seeing" meant, but they were drawn. Gradually, they trusted Jesus and obeyed. Their eyes were opened, and they served Jesus, but they did not understand fully until after His death and resurrection.

Each of us is the product of all that we have ever experienced. If we grew up free and privileged, never experiencing suffering or difficulty, we assume that everyone else had a life like that. If we grew up poor, or in a country ravaged by war, we think that others had the same experience. With the advent of television and social media, more people know how others live but, generally, our own day-to-day circumstances form us—except for faith in Jesus, which transforms us into new creatures.

Those born with or who develop life-changing disabilities often view life differently than their siblings who are born, and remain, healthy, although the latter may also be impacted by living with someone with health challenges. The healthy may develop more empathy. Living with a disability or with those who have a disability, as well as visiting the elderly, hospitalized, or incarcerated, affects who we are, how we relate to others, and our life perspective. But more importantly, it affects how we relate to God. Trials of life either draw us away from God or closer to Him. They make us loving and dependent on God or angry and independent of Him. We blame God or we ask Him for comfort.

God loves the poor, the incarcerated, the rich, the talented, the abused, and those with disabilities—equally. Yet those with health challenges or living in difficult circumstances may find it harder to love God. Or they may find it easier to call out to God and love Him because of their heartache and suffering. Numerous people who face what seems like insurmountable obstacles choose to trust God. Rather than harboring anger or bitterness, they live for Christ and draw others to God out of godly love.[17] Lives of disability, pain, and hardship can be extraordinarily rich, and inspiring to others.

Jesus beckons everyone to come to Him. The fallen, the broken, and the despairing—those in prisons, hospital rooms, nursing homes, and wartime trenches—often cry out to God, praying that He is listening. There is no place that His arm cannot reach. The ability to see as God desires us to see means that we want to understand as He does. We believe that God is compassionate and loving, despite life's many difficulties. Seeing and tasting that He is good requires some depth of spiritual understanding. Spiritually hearing, seeing, and tasting involves knowing God's love.

When God calls, individuals accept or turn away. Will you come and hear? Jesus said to them, "Come and you will see" (John 1:39a). God is Supreme—but He is not autocratic. Often people realize that there is nothing more that they themselves can do before accepting

---

[17] Numerous books and media about the following Christians exhibit God's love in action. Corrie ten Boom hid Jews during World War 2, survived a Nazi concentration camp, and promoted the gospel. Joni Eareckson Tada, a quadriplegic since her diving accident at seventeen, is a well-known Christian evangelist and author. Australian motivational speaker Nick Vujicic, born without limbs, is a husband, father, and one of the world's most inspirational people. World War 2 veteran and Olympic distance runner Louis Zamperini miraculously survived the Pacific Ocean and a Japanese prison camp. He helped spread the gospel after he was saved in 1949 at a Billy Graham crusade. Katherine and Jay Wolf's unwavering faith following Katherine's medical challenges and miracles demonstrates love and spiritual hope to a dying world.

God's call. We do not know the number of opportunities that each person will be given to accept and believe or turn away. God alone knows whether Jesus will affirm that we are His when our lives are over or when He returns.

Just as God called Israel to repent and be forgiven, He calls us today: "Then you will call on me and come and pray to me, and I will listen to you. You will seek me and find me when you seek me with all your heart" (Jer. 29:13). God calls when He sees that the heart is ready. The called must act within their will to answer. God is gracious, hears our cries, but He alone knows when we are ready to change. Those ready who hear His call see differently. They trust God more and become obedient. With God infusing their hearts with His Spirit, they see that they need God more than anything.

Through faith in Jesus, Christians know that they are saved through His death and resurrection. Their sins have been atoned for at the cross, and resurrection assures them of eternal life. They are comforted knowing, as Jesus teaches, that they may talk directly to God through Jesus as Mediator. Important in believing and trusting in Jesus and knowing God is the Bible. The Old Testament is crucial to understanding the New Testament. Jesus lived as a Jewish man and this is how He knew God, His Father. He knew and taught from the Hebrew Scripture as no person ever could. To understand Jesus's letters to the seven churches, the reader needs to know and understand at least the Ten Commandments and the Lord's Prayer (see Appendix II).

The Apostle John and Jesus's Revelation

The Apostle John

John was born around 6 AD in Bethsaida, Galilee, in the Roman Empire and died around 98–100 in Ephesus. He and his older brother James, sons of Zebedee and Salome, were two of the first four of Jesus's twelve apostles.[18] John, believed to have been the youngest apostle, is identified variously by church fathers as John of Patmos, the divine, the elder, the evangelist, the theologian, and the beloved disciple. It is likely that John wrote the fourth gospel, three letters, and Revelation.

John, part of Jesus's inner circle, loved and supported Him from the beginning, although he was first a disciple of John the Baptist. John was present at events where only one or two other apostles were present. John and Andrew are considered the two apostles who followed Jesus and spent the day with Him after hearing John the Baptist introduce Him as the "Lamb of God" (John 1:35–39). Called from lives of fishing on the Sea of Galilee alongside their father, John and his brother James joined Jesus, Peter, and Andrew to be "fishers of men" (Matt. 4:19). Jesus called the brothers James and John "sons of thunder" after He rebuked them for wanting to call down fire from heaven upon a Samaritan town that had rejected Him (Luke 9:51–56).

Only John, James, and Peter witnessed the raising of Jairus's daughter and were present at Jesus's transfiguration. They also witnessed Jesus's agony in Gethsemane. Jesus sent John and Peter into the city to prepare His last Passover meal, the Last Supper. At that meal, John, the disciple whom Jesus loved, sat next to Him. After Jesus's arrest, Peter and John followed Jesus into the high priest's palace, but John alone stood at the foot of the cross with the women as Jesus died. From the cross, Jesus entrusted John with His mother's care; this shows Jesus's esteem for John. John recorded how, after Mary Magdalene told him and Peter about the empty tomb, he arrived at the tomb first, but allowed Peter to be the first to enter (John 20:1–10), perhaps in deference to his age. John wrote that, until then, they had not understood scripture and how Jesus must rise from the dead. Afterwards, Peter and John believed in Jesus as the Messiah and were pivotal in founding and building the church.

---

[18] "John the Apostle," accessed October 21, 2019, https://en.wikipedia.org/wiki/John_the_Apostle.

John's brother James the Great (or Greater) was martyred in 44 AD, ten years after Stephen was stoned to death. John lived at least fifty years after his brother died. His dedication to Jesus was unsurpassed. According to *Foxe's Book of Martyrs*, John founded all seven churches of Revelation: Laodicea, Pergamum, Philadelphia, Sardis, Smyrna, Thyatira, and Ephesus. John was arrested in Ephesus and sent to Rome, where he miraculously escaped without injury from a pot of boiling oil. The emperor Domitian later banished him to the Isle of Patmos, where he wrote Revelation. After being released from Patmos, John spent the rest of his life in and around Ephesus.[19]

John's gospel ends with an interesting twist. Jesus, in a final appearance after His resurrection, directed His seven apostles, whose nighttime fishing on Galilee had produced nothing, to find fish. After breakfast, John followed, as Jesus spoke to Peter:

> Peter turned and saw the disciple whom Jesus loved following them, the one who had been reclining at table close to him and had said, "Lord, who is it that is going to betray you?" When Peter saw him he said to Jesus, "Lord, what about this man?" Jesus said to him, "If it is my will that he remain until I come, what is that to you? You follow me!" So the saying spread among the brothers that this disciple was not to die; yet Jesus did not say to him that he was not to die, but, "If it is my will that he remain until I come, what is that to you?"
>
> This is the disciple who is bearing witness about these things, and who has written these things, and we know that his testimony is true.
>
> Now there are also many other things that Jesus did. Were every one of them to be written, I suppose that the world itself could not contain the books that would be written. (John 21:20–25)

---

[19] John Foxe, *Foxe's Book of Martyrs* (Alachua, FL: Bridge-Logos, 2001), 7.

This resurrection event speaks to more than the apostles' loyalty or their fishing for people to follow Christ. It illustrates fallen human nature. Peter inferred and told others that John would live until Jesus returned, despite His rebuke to concern himself only with his business. Jesus had not yet returned but appeared to John in the visions of Revelation. In a sense, John did live to see Jesus return, or at least to talk of His return.

John outlived all the apostles, dying around 98 AD.[20] He was the one entrusted with receiving and sharing Jesus's revelation. John was instrumental in church growth from its beginning and will be to its end. His writings are rich because he was present for all of Jesus's ministry, cared for His mother, and was delegated by Jesus in the power of the Holy Spirit to deliver His only words that were purposefully intended to be included in God's Word. John knew more of what happened and what was written and dispersed during Christianity's monumental first century than any other person.

Jesus's Revelation

Although the apocalyptic genre is elusive and frightening to some, Revelation is more than first-century Jewish-Christian apocalyptic literature. It is God's revelation of the future to humankind, but it does not follow a chronological order. Revelation cannot be bound to one human interpretation. God alone knows its meaning, intricacies, and end.

The only direct words that Jesus told John to write and distribute to the church were revealed in a vision to John. We may think that he was the one given this honor because he was the only living apostle at the time, but John was purposefully chosen by God before the beginning of time to receive these prophetic visions, write, and send the whole book of Revelation to seven churches. Despite his frailty, John unequivocally had proved his trustworthiness and faithful endurance through at least seven decades.

Jesus knew that John would present His message well, despite

---

[20] Ibid.

his being persecuted at an old age. For John, the responsibility must have been formidable. Anyone who has read Revelation knows how complicated and difficult it is to understand. To some, the book is simply too overwhelming; to others, it entices and challenges academic prowess. Countless interpretations, theories, and prophesied dates and times of Revelation's perplexing visions have been proven wrong.

Some conclude that Revelation spoke only to seven communities in Asia Minor and that every reference to time in it must be taken literally, as those communities did. The book, however, is especially relevant to Christian persecution; early first-century Christians suffered under Roman rule and the domination of emperors, including Domitian. With increasing persecution of Christians, decreasing morality, and increasing lawlessness, the Bible's final book takes on even greater meaning for twenty-first-century Christians. Most believe that Revelation is as relevant for the church today as it was for first-century Christians, but its historical context must be considered. Jesus warned that nothing is to be added to or taken away from this book.

The main message to the seven first-century churches was for Christians to hold firm to their faith and not to conform to Greco-Roman society or assimilate into the Roman imperial cult. They should speak and act in the manner that Jesus had taught His followers through scripture while He was alive and in Christian documents after that (i.e., the scrolls of the gospels, Acts, the epistles, and Revelation). Doing so would ensure their eternal well-being. God's wrath would fall upon the disobedient.

Understanding Revelation's concept of eternal security through Christ is crucial. Although Jesus's revelation tells what will happen, and we know that the Bible is reliable and valid,[21] it does not say how or when events will unfold. The seven letters describe how Christians

---

[21] What has been passed down as scripture has been shown to be highly accurate and extremely close to what was first written, as proven by the Dead Sea Scrolls in recent years. Errors are few and usually scribal, although the scribes faithfully, patiently, and painstakingly copied each book. Scribes worked diligently and fastidiously copying each jot and tittle for the sake of the gospel.

are to be Christ's body or faithful community while preparing for what will eventually take place. Portions of Revelation mirror portions of Jeremiah, Ezekiel, Daniel, Zechariah, Matthew, Mark, Luke, and 1 and 2 Thessalonians, but Revelation in its entirety provides a full, yet obscure, picture of the events that will come to pass.

John obediently wrote what Jesus told him to write. Those who delivered the letters (and most likely the whole of Revelation) to the seven churches on scrolls (without chapter or verse numbers) would likely have taken the traditional postal route, beginning with Ephesus, and ending with Laodicea, that is, the order in which they occur in Revelation. Most churches from then on would have had access to Revelation unless their bishops kept it from them.

Early dispute about Revelation did not keep it out of the canon, despite efforts of the Laodicean Synod in 363/4 AD. The earliest mention of Revelation's canonical status dates to the Muratorian Canon (or Fragment), a Latin list of New Testament books believed to have originated from a 170 AD Greek manuscript. Melito, bishop of Sardis (170 AD), wrote a commentary on Revelation, but it is not extant. Justin Martyr and Irenaeus also refer to Revelation, declaring the apostle John its author.[22]

Revelation reflects the Jewish/Christian culture of the first century and has a twofold purpose. First, it provides, mainly through its seven letters, a picture of what a healthy church looks like compared to a dying church. It provides a synopsis of what it means to follow Jesus. Second, it describes major future apocalyptic events that will unfold as the world we know ends and ushers in Christ's second coming. *The Greatest Love* emphasizes the first purpose. The church letters, read with faith and a desire to be within God's will, reveal what is necessary to be a Christian. Everyone who sincerely seeks spiritual wisdom will have it breathed into them by the Holy Spirit. They will be motivated to know God's Word better by consulting concordant Bible

---

[22] Joseph M. Holden and Norman Geisler, *The Popular Handbook of Archaeology and the Bible* (Eugene, OR: Harvest House, 2013), 173.

passages and using tools[23] that reinforce God's Word and Jesus's overall message to Christians and the world.

What to Expect from the Letters to the Churches

The next seven chapters focus on Revelation's seven letters, with one chapter designated to each letter. Together these letters reveal Jesus's teaching on picking up one's cross and following Him. They are His final and direct reminder of how Christians are to honor God so that they inherit eternal life.

Archaeological excavations of the seven ancient cities that housed the seven churches show that these cities had much in common. Most striking was the acropolis, a hilltop often central to the city where temples, castles, and other major buildings stood. Of note were an agora (the central open marketplace in ancient Greek cities), a cardo (the main street in ancient Roman cities), large outdoor theaters, gymnasiums and stadiums (popular because of Greek/Olympic sports), bath houses, brothels, and private homes.

Each city was influenced by its Greco-Roman past and Greek and Roman gods were openly worshipped. As part of the Roman imperial cult, citizens were also required to worship Roman emperors by burning and offering incense in their honor. Temples built to honor the Greek and Roman gods were also centers of drunkenness, orgies, animal sacrifice, and sometimes mutilation. Meat from sacrifices to the gods was often shared with the needy. Most Christians were poor and hungry, but they would not have attended religious rituals that conflicted with their beliefs.

---

[23] The popular literary device of chiastic structure is one tool that shows patterns in words or ideas. Chiastic structure is reflexive, somewhat like a mirror image, and sometimes juxtaposed. The term *chiasm* or *chiasmus* comes from *chi*, the twenty-second letter of the Greek alphabet. Revelation, in its parts and as a whole, contains various chiastic patterns. Appendix III outlines a simple chiasm of the seven letters, showing how each letter and church is both aligned with and contrasted to others. Jesus's commendations and rebukes to the seven churches help readers understand His message of salvation by faith and transformation through Him.

It is to seven Greco-Roman communities in Asia Minor that Jesus purposely sent His only, yet final, words to the church and to the world. These letters are pivotal to understanding Jesus's message because they outline His expectations not only for their communities but for His church. Christians have been, are, and will continue to be buoyed up in their faith of a loving God who assures them of eternity with Him in a perfected world to come. Revelation is a sacred ending to a holy book.

The following map shows the Isle of Patmos and the seven churches of Revelation with respect to their location in Asia Minor (Anatolia, modern-day Turkey). The order of the letters within Revelation is most likely the order in which they were delivered. The map shows approximately Laodicea's location between Hierapolis and the mound which is ancient Colossae.

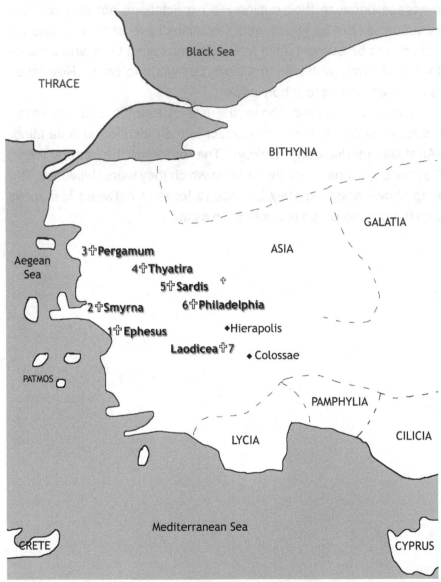

The Seven Churches of Revelation.

Section III

God's Love

I, John, your brother and partner in the tribulation and the kingdom and the patient endurance that are in Jesus, was on the island called Patmos on account of the word of God and the testimony of Jesus. I was in the Spirit on the Lord's day, and I heard behind me a loud voice like a trumpet saying, "Write what you see in a book and send it to the seven churches, to Ephesus and to Smyrna and to Pergamum and to Thyatira and to Sardis and to Philadelphia and to Laodicea." (Rev. 1:9–11)

Statue to Atatürk, Izmir, Turkey.[24]

[24] Prof. Mehmet Özdoğan, *Talks on Atatürk: Atatürk and Turkish Archaeology*, October 31, 2018, accessed August 3, 2020, https://en.iae.org.tr/Event-Detail/ Ataturk-and-Turkish-Archaeology-Prof-Mehmet-Ozdogan/136. Kemal Atatürk was the founding father and first president of the Republic of Turkey (1923–1938), where most cities and towns have a statue in his honor. The biblical world is much richer for the archaeological work done in Anatolia: "Atatürk's Turkey regarded archaeology not as a mere tool to fill the museums with artefacts, but rather as a field of science that enabled the documentation and understanding of the past."

CHAPTER 3

Ephesus—Greatest Love Lost

To the angel of the church in Ephesus write: "The words of him who holds the seven stars in his right hand, who walks among the seven golden lampstands.

"I know your works, your toil and your patient endurance, and how you cannot bear with those who are evil, but have tested those who call themselves apostles and are not, and found them to be false. I know you are enduring patiently and bearing up for my name's sake, and you have not grown weary. But I have this against you, that you have abandoned the love you had at first. Remember therefore from where you have fallen; repent, and do the works you did at first. If not, I will come to you and remove your lampstand from its place, unless you repent. Yet this you have: you hate the works of the Nicolaitans, which I also hate. He who has an ear, let him hear what the Spirit says to the churches. To the one who conquers I will grant to eat of the tree of life, which is in the paradise of God." (Rev. 2:1–7)

Jesus referred to the seven churches of Asia Minor as the seven lampstands. Seven, one of four Jewish perfect numbers, represents completeness and spiritual perfection. Jesus's light shines brightly through Christians, who are called to be light in the world's darkness. When these churches were first instituted, all seven projected the light of Jesus's love and truth brightly for all to see.

Where in the World Is Ephesus?

Ephesus, two miles southwest of present-day Selçuk in Izmir province, Turkey, and less than twenty miles north of cruise-ship port Kusadasi, was designated a UNESCO World Heritage Site in 2015. It is easy to imagine Ephesus as a bustling city in the first century AD, complete with a magnificent harbor. Due to a huge buildup of silt, Ephesus now lies uninhabited, about six miles from the Aegean Sea near the mouth of the Cayster River.

Paul is usually credited with planting the church in Ephesus around 52 AD, after he had visited Corinth on his second missionary journey (Acts 18:19), but according to Foxe, John planted all seven churches. Closest to the Isle of Patmos, Ephesus likely received its letter first. The fourth largest city of the Roman Empire, Ephesus is considered by scholars to have been the most cosmopolitan of the seven cities.[25]

According to tradition, Ephesus is where John cared for Jesus's mother, Mary, until her death, and where she is buried. It is believed that John spent his last years in and around Ephesus, after his release from exile on Patmos. Also according to tradition, John's remains were buried at the Basilica of St. John in Ephesus, but it is not known whether he was martyred or died of natural causes.[26]

History and Archaeology

Excavations show that Ephesus was inhabited from about 6,000 BC. Recent scholarship supports that it was built on a Bronze Age city, perhaps under Ahhiyawan rule, according to Hittite sources. Ceramic pots discovered in 1954 close to the ruins of the Basilica

---

[25] Colin J. Hemer, *The Letters to the Seven Churches of Asia in Their Local Setting*, Biblical Resource Series (Grand Rapids, MI: William B. Eerdmans, 2001), 35.
[26] Archaeological sites in and around Ephesus are based on these traditional beliefs about John and Mary, mother of Jesus.

of St. John come from a burial ground from the Mycenaean Era, 1,500 to 1,400 BC.[27]

Ancient Ephesus was built in the tenth century BC by Attic and Ionian Greek colonists as one of twelve cities of the Ionian League. It was re-founded by Lysimachus (also Lysimachos), a general of Alexander the Great, in the fourth century BC and continued to flourish until 133 BC, when Asia Minor was incorporated into the Roman Empire. Strategically located on the Mediterranean Sea at the junction of three major roads, one of which ran across Asia Minor into Syria, Ephesus in the first century AD was a wealthy commercial city and capital of Asia Minor. Its harbor was regularly dredged of its silt, until the city declined in the third and fourth centuries.

Ephesus was noted for its Temple of Artemis, Greek goddess of the hunt and fertility, also known as the Roman goddess Diana. Archaeological excavations began in 1862 when John Turtle Wood, a British railway engineer, began to search for the temple, which he found seven years later.[28] The temple was one of the Seven Wonders of the Ancient World.[29]

Completed around the eighth century BC, the temple was destroyed by a flood in the seventh century, rebuilt with the assistance of King Croesus in approximately 550 BC, and destroyed by arson in 356 BC. Refusing help, even from Alexander the Great, the Ephesians began work on a third, enlarged temple in 323 BC. They wanted Artemis for themselves, although temples were dedicated to her elsewhere in the region.[30]

People from all over Asia flocked to Ephesus to visit this great temple and to worship Artemis, the Anatolian goddess Cybele, and

---

[27] "Ephesus," accessed August 13, 2018, https://en.wikipedia.org/wiki/Ephesus.

[28] Mark Wilson, *Biblical Turkey: A Guide to the Jewish and Christian Sites of Asia Minor,* 3rd ed. (Istanbul, Turkey: Ege Yayinlari, 2014), 205. Some artifacts are housed in the British Museum in London.

[29] "Temple of Artemis," accessed January 23, 2020, https://newworldencyclopedia. org/entry/Temple_of_Artemis. This temple outshone the walls and Hanging Gardens of ancient Babylon, the Colossus of Rhodes, the Olympian statue of Zeus, and the pyramids and tomb of Mausolus, according to Philo of Byzantium.

[30] "Temple of Artemis," accessed January 22, 2020, https://en.wikipedia.org/wiki/ Temple_of_Artemis.

as many as twelve other gods, while participating in pagan rituals. Every spring thousands pilgrimaged to Ephesus for an annual festival in Artemis's honor, with celebrations and parties involving a parade to the temple, where some young men caught in the frenzy of the festivities castrated themselves so that they could serve at the temple.

Artemis's many breasts have been associated with a meteorite with breastlike bumps that had fallen from the sky. Reference is made to Artemis and a sacred stone falling from the sky in Acts 19:35. In 2020, only one column of the temple in her honor still stood after its destruction in 262 AD by the Goths. Metal multi-breasted replicas of Artemis are sold all throughout Turkey and beyond.

The buildings and artifacts unearthed show the affluence of Ephesian life: the 12,000-scroll Library of Celsus, the agora, the odeum (where city council met), a commercial trade center, the water place, and Curetes and Harbour Streets (two long streets lined with monuments and buildings). Other ruins include a monument to Nike, temples of Hadrian and Domitian, the Grand Theatre, the Marble Road, a large gymnasium, the Trajan Fountain, a stadium, a brothel, public baths, ornamental gates and fountains, the Basilica of St. John, and the Houses on the Slopes (five lavish residential homes, two of which had heated bathrooms).

When Emperor Augustus replaced Pergamum with Ephesus in 27 BC as the capital of proconsular Asia, Ephesus became even more prosperous, second only to Rome: it was the seat of government and a popular commercial center. During the Roman period, its population reached approximately two hundred thousand to two hundred fifty thousand inhabitants, making it one of the largest cities in Roman Asia Minor.

Inwardly Digesting Revelation 2:1–7

Revelation 2:1

> To the angel of the church in Ephesus write: The words
> of him who holds the seven stars in his right hand,
> who walks among the seven golden lampstands.

Jesus holds the seven stars in His right hand and walks among the seven golden lampstands. The seven stars are the angels of the seven churches and the seven lampstands are the seven churches (Rev. 1:20). Individually these seven churches are spiritually imperfect, but as Christ's body they are made complete and spiritually whole in Him. They represent the universal Christian church. That Jesus holds the stars in His right hand and walks among the lampstands symbolizes His omnipotence. He is also omniscient, knowing everything that each angel and church did, and will, do. The angels and churches are God's Spirit alive in Christians and in Christ's church.

Jesus's walking among the churches indicates His presence within His church, His spiritual body, after His death. There is no extant account that Jesus ever walked in this area during his lifetime, but, as God, His Spirit is everywhere, although He sits at the right hand of God in heaven. God's mysteries cannot be fully known or understood, but Christians believe that the Holy Spirit came at Pentecost, fifty days after Jesus's resurrection and ten days after His ascension. They know that the Holy Spirit resides in every Christian. The church in Ephesus knew this. John, Paul, and others in the early church would have talked about such things as they walked the roads in and around Ephesus.

Revelation 2:2

> I know your works, your toil and your patient
> endurance, and how you cannot bear with those who
> are evil but have tested those who call themselves
> apostles and are not and found them to be false.

Jesus knows the works, the efforts, and the endurance of the Ephesians. He knows their history of not tolerating the evil around them and how they persevered for their faith. Jesus knows those who pretend to be Christians but are not. The early church in Ephesus had scrutinized all the letters and church leaders that came its way and it rejected some of them. It had to, because wrong trust could have meant death. Jesus tells the Ephesian church that it had done this well. He praises it for its hard work, patient endurance, and ability to discern false doctrine. This church had a reputation of working hard, rooting out heresy, and upholding the truth.

Revelation 2:3

> *I know you are enduring patiently and bearing up for*
> *my name's sake, and you have not grown weary.*

Jesus compliments the Ephesian church for being patient, enduring, and bearing up for His name. This was an accomplishment, considering all that they had endured as Christians in a pagan, idolatrous environment. Jesus commends them for their strength. They were doing many things right, despite the sordid pagan rituals and idolatry of their culture.

Revelation 2:4

> *But I have this against you, that you have abandoned*
> *the love you had at first.*

It is ironic that the church known for testing apostles and finding error did itself err due to its lack of love for God, breaking the greatest commandment which Jesus taught, and which Christians must hold in tandem with the truth of the gospel if it is to be faithful. Loving God first is *the* most important of God's commands to the church. The Ephesian church erred on this basic, yet most-important tenet of their faith. Christians must love God first, then each other and everyone else.

In his letter to the Ephesians, dated around 62 AD, Paul sent them spiritual blessings in Christ, saying how those in that church were, in love, predestined for adoption as sons through Jesus. He spoke of their inheritance according to Jesus, who works all things according to the council of His will. Paul thanked God as he had heard of the Ephesians' faith in the Lord Jesus and their love for all the saints (Eph. 1:15). Paul's letter, however, hints that the Ephesian church may have had trials. He asked God to give them a spirit of wisdom and revelation in the knowledge of Him so that the eyes of their hearts could be enlightened to know the hope to which they were called (Eph. 1:15–23). He cautioned them against wrongdoing, while giving thanks and praying for them several times. In Ephesians 3:14–20, Paul prayed that the Ephesian church would be "rooted and grounded in love," with strength to understand and "know the love of Christ," which is only possible through the indwelling power of the Holy Spirit. Later Paul urged the Ephesians to walk in a manner worthy of their calling, "speaking the truth in love" so that they might grow in Christ's likeness (Eph. 4:15).

Revelation 2:5

> *Remember therefore from where you have fallen; repent, and do the works you did at first. If not, I will come to you and remove your lampstand from its place, unless you repent.*

Jesus asks the Ephesian church to remember where they once were and what they had once believed. When Paul had written them thirty years earlier, they seemed to love God first. They were God's and God was theirs. Their works were done on His behalf out of love for Him. Jesus reminds them to think about what they may be losing, that which is most important—their faith, which included heaven. He asks them to think about how they should live and be remembered. Jesus implores them to repent and love God first, as they once did. If they did not love God first, their church would die, and people would be eternally lost. If the Ephesians did not repent, there would be no church in Ephesus; Jesus would remove their lampstand. This church would then be dark and lost, just like the city in which it lived.

Revelation 2:6

> *Yet this you have: you hate the works of the Nicolaitans, which I also hate.*

The Nicolaitans mixed pagan rituals, temple worship, and sexual immorality with Christianity because they thought that the physical body did not impact their spirits. But Jesus taught that it did. Some Nicolaitans considered themselves Christian, but the Ephesian Christians knew that they were not.

There is hope: the Ephesian church hated some of what God hates. It hated the works and liberality of those Christians who compromised their values and ate food sacrificed to idols. It detested animal strangulation and rampant sexual immorality. It likely would have seen the letter to Antioch sent from the Jerusalem Council (48–49 AD) to Gentile Christians that described how eating food sacrificed to idols and sexual immorality are an abomination to God (Acts 15:20, 29; 21:25).

Revelation 2:7

> *He who has an ear, let him hear what the Spirit says to the churches. To the one who conquers I will grant to eat of the tree of life, which is in the paradise of God.*

Common to Revelation are the terms *conquerors* and *overcomers*, which refer to those who will be with Jesus for eternity. Conquerors, in their own will through the power of the Holy Spirit, overcome the temptation of their own flesh and overcome the world. Jesus will grant the Ephesian conquerors to eat of the tree of life in the paradise of God, referring directly to creation and the garden of Eden (Gen. 2:9; 3:22) and the River of Life in the New Jerusalem (Rev. 22:1–2). The tree of life symbolizes eternal life, heaven.

The "holy" place of Artemis was referred to as the tree-shrine, a place of asylum for anyone fearing for their life. Excavations in Ephesus support that successive temples were built on the site of this sacred tree. Christians in the first century associated the tree with the cross of Christ.[31] They knew that Jesus spoke of the tree as bearing perfect fruit in the garden of Eden before the fall and in the future new heaven and new earth because they knew scripture. They knew that every tree is known by its fruit, as Jesus said:

> Either make the tree good and its fruit good, or make the tree bad and its fruit bad, for the tree is known by its fruit. You brood of vipers! How can you speak good, when you are evil? For out of the abundance of the heart the mouth speaks. The good person out of his good treasure brings forth good, and the evil person out of his evil treasure brings forth evil. I tell you, on the day of judgment people will give account for every careless word they speak, for by your words you will be justified, and by your works you will be condemned. (Matt. 12:33–37)

Jesus calls for the Ephesians to conquer, to overcome, to get at the root of what is causing their problem, and to defeat it. Jesus may be saying something like this: "Look to me, you first loved me. Why don't you love me the same anymore? Maybe it is a matter of needing a rest, some quiet time, time away from this place where there is so much sin, time to come to me, be refreshed and nourished. Time for you to pray, read the Bible, and meditate on it. You hate the sin of the Nicolaitans as my Father does. Come, allow me to build you up, as we love one another as our Father loves us."

> Therefore be imitators of God, as beloved children.
> And walk in love, as Christ loved us and gave himself up for us, a fragrant offering and sacrifice to God. (Eph. 5:1–2)

---

[31] Hemer, *The Letters to the Seven Churches,* 41–47.

Ephesus was one of the earliest churches founded in Asia Minor. Other churches and church leaders likely grew out of it. The city's strategic geographic and maritime location at the juncture of three main roads facilitated the spread of the gospel. The good news of Jesus Christ was probably spread as easily from the port and along the roads as goods and information were shared. Due to its prominence as a port city, Ephesus controlled a large network of roads.

In Acts 19:10, Luke reports that Paul had preached the gospel to Jews and Greeks for about two years, until all the residents in Asia had heard it. Paul's strategy of setting up in major cities and sending co-workers into surrounding areas was aided by the networks of roads in those cities that he chose. It was important that the Ephesians know God's truth and be grounded in love, loving God first with their whole hearts. Getting everything else right was useless if their love for God had died. Orthodoxy and hard work are futile unless the gospel is spread in godly love.

Jesus told the church that it had abandoned its first love. Why was there such a difference between Paul's and John's letters? The thirty-plus years between Paul's writing of Ephesians in the 60s and John's writing of Revelation in the 90s suggest that a great change had occurred in the Ephesian church between these two letters.

Plagues, famines, and wars can change the world almost instantaneously. We should not be surprised about the drastic change in the Ephesian church between Paul's and John's letters. People are lost, and saved, in the blink of an eye. This church was in dire trouble, but if it heeded Jesus's warning, repented, and returned to teaching the truth with the love of God, it could return to its former good standing.

Jesus's rebuke about losing their first love must have shocked the Ephesians after the positive comments before and after the reprimand. Abandoning their first love had eternal consequences. God commands Christians to love Him first and then to love all others as they love Him. Did abandoning their first love mean that they had lost their love for God? Is Jesus saying that they no longer had any love for God, or had they taken Him out of first place? Were they merely going through the motions of being a church? Were their senses dulled from fighting their enemies? Did they fear for their safety? Or were they serving another master?

Despite being steeped in a pagan culture, and perhaps because of it, the church in Ephesus was strong and faithful in its early years. Paul had built up church members and given them advice as to how to keep their faith. In addition to battling Greek and Roman pagan rituals and worship, they also battled the Roman imperial cult, angry Jewish leaders, and tradesmen who were attempting to make a living from items related to pagan worship and rituals such as metal statues of Artemis. They also struggled against drunkenness, prostitution, and licentiousness.

The book of Acts, probably known to the church in Ephesus, warned of the sin associated with Artemis and temple worship. The riot in the Grand Theater was the result of Paul's teachings on idolatry (Acts 19:21–41). The situation escalated quickly because what Paul said detracted from the silversmiths' efforts to sell Artemis statues. One silversmith, Demetrius, caused a group of tradesmen to riot when he said that their goddess was dishonored and their livelihoods endangered by Paul's teachings about Jesus. Acts 18 and 19 record other misunderstandings. Apollos, an Alexandrian Jew and eloquent speaker competent in scripture, spoke accurately about Jesus, but he only knew of baptism through John. Paul, then, was aware of early church writings warning church leaders to be vigilant against false teaching, as he himself wrote to fight false teachers and their many heresies.

According to tradition, Timothy, first bishop of Ephesus and recipient of two letters from Paul, died in 97 AD, just two days after he received a severe beating by the Ephesians because he had reproved them about idolatry at a pagan ritual.[32] His death, likely just after Revelation was written, coupled with decades of Christian

---

[32] Foxe, *Foxe's Book of Martyrs*, 10.

unease after Paul had precipitated the silversmith riot in the theater, may provide some clue as to the changes that had occurred in the Ephesian church. Jesus said that they had not grown weary; perhaps they cowered because of threats of harm from the pagans. Maybe their hearts became hard because they were angered by paganism and false teaching. Some may have softened their language to be less conspicuous. Whatever happened as they fought the sin around them, they lost their love for those they were to love.

The Grand Theater, Ephesus, site of the riot in Acts 19.

The First Love Is the Greatest

Hear, O Israel: The LORD our God, the LORD is one. You shall love the LORD your God with all your heart and with all your soul and with all your might. And these words that I command you today shall be on your heart. You shall teach them diligently to your children and shall talk of them when you sit in your house, and when you walk by the way, and when you lie down, and when you rise. (Deut. 6:4–7)

The greatest commandment given to Israel and taught by Jesus is the Shema, from the Hebrew word for *hear.* The Lord God alone is Israel's God. There is only one true God, and Jesus, His Son, is equal in the Godhead with Father and Holy Spirit.

Our first commandment is to love God with all that we are. Deuteronomy 6:4–7 is the basic tenet of both Judaism and Christianity. Three gospels (Matthew, Mark, and Luke) record Jesus's response to the Pharisees, a scribe, and a lawyer: each time He quoted the Shema. Jesus responded to the Pharisees:

> You shall love the Lord your God with all your heart and with all your soul and with all your mind. This is the great and first commandment. And a second is like it: You shall love your neighbour as yourself. On these two commandments depend all the Law and the Prophets. (Matt. 22:36–40)

Jesus answered the scribe:

> The most important is, Hear, O Israel: The Lord our God, the Lord is one. And you shall love the Lord your God with all your heart and with all your soul and with all your mind and with all your strength. The second is this: You shall love your neighbour as yourself. There is no other commandment greater than these. (Mark 12:29–31)

In Luke, the basic tenet for faithful living comes through the Parable of the Good Samaritan:

> And behold, a lawyer stood up to put Him to the test, saying, "Teacher what shall I do to inherit eternal life?" He said to him, "What is written in the Law? How do you read it?" And he answered, "You shall love the Lord your God with all your heart and with all your soul and with all your strength and with all your

mind, and your neighbor as yourself." And He said to him, "You have answered correctly; do this and you will live." (Luke 10:25–28)

Jesus turned the lawyer's question back to him. After the lawyer answered correctly, Jesus tells him to do that and he will have eternal life, but the lawyer's seeking to justify himself shows his insincerity (vv. 29–37).

These passages illustrate how some who should be wise and understand the scripture are not. Jesus's answers came readily from the Hebrew Scripture. To love the Lord your God means having faith in and delighting in Him above everything else. Matthew, Mark, and Luke include loving with the heart, the center of one's being and will. They include loving with the soul, that immaterial part of the human being that lives eternally. The three gospels add loving with the mind, which Deuteronomy does not contain: the ability to reason and to think logically. Only Matthew adds *strength,* which is similar to the word *might* used in Deuteronomy, that is, how a person uses his or her whole person in total devotion to God. Clearly, we are to love God with all that we are.

The gospel of John approaches love and the command to love differently:

> When he had gone out, Jesus said, "Now is the Son of Man glorified, and God is glorified in him. If God is glorified in him, God will also glorify him in himself, and glorify him at once. Little children, yet a little while I am with you. You will seek me, and just as I said to the Jews, so now I also say to you, 'Where I am going you cannot come.' A new commandment I give to you, that you love one another: just as I have loved you, you also are to love one another. By this all people will know that you are my disciples, if you have love for one another." (John 13:31–35)

John's gospel, however, does not refer to the Shema but to Leviticus 19:18: "You shall not take vengeance or bear a grudge against the sons of your own people, but you shall love your neighbor as yourself: I am the LORD." Jesus teaches how Christians are to treat one another based on the fundamental principle of God's law as expressed in the Hebrew Scripture, often referred to and quoted in the New Testament.

Jesus gave this *new* commandment to His eleven apostles after Judas had left the table of the last supper. John 13:31–32 echoes Isaiah 49:3, in which Jesus's glorification is tied to His death. In this way, John links Jesus's love for humanity to His ultimate sacrificial death upon the cross: Jesus willingly gave His life for everyone.

The church in Ephesus at first was obedient to this command to love God first, but at the writing of Revelation, it was disobedient.

Abandoning God's Love and Goodness

At one time God was first on the minds and in the hearts of Ephesian Christians. We do not know if they succumbed to pagan, Roman, or Jewish political pressure or threat of harm. Often, persecution causes Christians to love and lean on God more, not less.

Prideful and incredibly competitive, Ephesus was successful even in its plight to rebuild Artemis's temple for the third time. It always put itself first. It fought to keep its harbor and strategic location, until the silt won out. Although it was not the first Christian center in Asia Minor, it grew fast. Ephesus was also idolatrous. Not only were pagan and Roman gods and emperors worshipped, but the human body, sexual pleasure, knowledge, health, and wealth were also worshipped. Jesus warns that it is dangerous to love comfort, work, or pleasure before God. When we do not put God first, we sin.

Whatever the reason, God did not come first in the Ephesian church. Maybe it was prideful, like the city. Maybe it grew too fast, members had too much work to do, and threats of physical harm caused them to question their priorities. Maybe pride in their accomplishments led to overconfidence and insensitivity to God's love. Perhaps they resented God for not stepping in when pagans bullied, rioted, and brutalized them. Jesus's warning that their lampstand might be removed, however, shows how seriously they had compromised their faith. The church in Ephesus died because it did not put God first. By abandoning God, it denied its first love. For whatever reasons, the Ephesian church put something or someone else in God's place.[33]

Ephesus in Our Time

Many Christians today are poor financially yet rich spiritually. In contrast are those rich financially who dismiss spiritual wealth because being self-sufficient, comfortable, and contented are lofty goals. Christians who believe that they are saved and heaven-bound because of their own and their church's tithes and good works may be deceived as the first-century Ephesian church was. If God is not loved first, tithes and works are futile.

The letter to the church in Ephesus is written to the comfortable who believe that they are part of Christ's Body. It has much to teach those in affluent parts of the world who profess to be Christians, because in many aspects the Ephesian church was teaching the truth, but in the most important aspect it was wrong. At first, this church had right thinking and probably had little organization. It grew out of the need to feel God's presence and His love, to answer His call to follow Jesus, and to evangelize. From Paul's letter sent to the early Ephesian church, we can infer that it was orthodox.

After a time, it became organized and hosted three councils, the first in 190 AD, with Polycrates, bishop of Ephesus. If organization

---

[33] Incarcerated men and women sometimes find it easy to look past language, skin color, economic status, education level, and religion. Some discern what is ultimately most important once other freedoms have been removed. In discussions about the Bible, some show genuine interest and a remarkable understanding of biblical concepts, for example, putting alcohol, drugs, family, and a mate before God is not what God expects. These realize that their sins result from their own inherent sinful nature. Many inmates want a changeless God who will help them change and remain changed.

---

becomes the raison d'être, God is not placed first. When this happens, we question who or what is loved first. It is like a self-serving marriage: the institution is desired, not relationship with the other person. Well-organized institutions may become complacent and prideful. Over time, they can fall into the trap of doing things in a regular way, time, and place. With respect to a church, it is easy to be tricked into thinking that God is not present all the time but only in the church building at set worship times and in the regular format. Similarly, some regard religious dress as a baptism, reminding them of their Christian responsibility. Christians must be mindful of the dangers of both practices.

Christians are Christians twenty-four hours a day, seven days a week, regardless of dress or location. No Christian attends church regularly yet lives sinfully during the remaining hours. When being Christian means that one worships for a specified time per week in a designated place, dressed in a specific way, it is easy to infer that God can be evaded. Gradually, relationship with God may deteriorate and faith become questionable. Worshipping an institution and what it deems to be right is spiritually quite dangerous.

Everyone can learn much from the Ephesian church: it is easy to become self-reliant and prideful without depending on God. It is easy to fall into human institutional snares, despite kind, loving, and well-meaning leaders and/or members. Meetings, liturgy, and social events are good, but if Christians do not love God first, as they are commanded to do, and as Jesus teaches, they can easily fall from belief into unbelief.

Terra cotta pipes in the corner of this ancient affluent Ephesian home.

The letter to Ephesus is a wake-up call for all comfortable Christians. Because their worldly needs are being met, they are in danger of never having put God first, and/or of being drawn away from the church by the world, the devil, and their own sinful desires. The Bible asserts that it is easier for a rich man to go through the eye of a needle than to get into the Kingdom of God, but it is not impossible. With God, all things are possible.

Those who love God before all else, and follow Jesus, are part of the Christian church throughout the world. The Ephesian letter shows that it is possible to lose one's salvation (or justification). It also shows how easily the saved (or justified) can lose opportunities for further sanctification. Faith must be carefully protected. Christians can be drawn into sin as the Ephesian church was, or they may persevere and conquer, overcome, and be victorious in Christ (Rev. 2:7b). The Bible commands all Christians to constantly examine themselves against God's perfect way so that they can confess, repent, and be forgiven when they sin.

The Ephesian church failed miserably. Its doors have been closed since 262 AD, but not all its people may be lost. It is possible that some Ephesian Christians patiently endured to the end of their lives and overcame their sin, in Christ. Only Jesus knows why Ephesus was the first church to be addressed. It was likely because of its loss of love. Love is the reason that God created. Love is the reason that God sent Jesus to be the perfect sacrifice. Love is the reason that we turn to God when we do. But dishonest love is a contradiction of terms. If we say that we love someone and lie to them, we do not love them. Honesty is basic to love, but it is not always highly valued today. Dishonesty contravenes the ninth commandment. It is easier sometimes to tell a lie than the truth, but when lies are told, it is the devil and/or the world who is speaking, not someone of God. Jesus repeatedly teaches the importance of keeping God's laws and commands.

Without God's love, we are dead, because all worldly love culminates in physical death. Godly love resulting from faith in Christ is the reason for righteous Christian living. It ensures eternal life and provides perfect love while we are in the world. The church, built on God's love, must love God first and then others, as it is loved. It must teach the truth in love to a dying world; otherwise, people will perish. The church in Ephesus failed to love. It lost its lamp and perished. Churches can fall like Ephesus did. They must heed the words of Christ and depend on the Holy Spirit and the Bible to keep them accountable. Christians must hold their churches accountable. Leaders must teach God's truth in love yet not be judgmental. Keeping to God's path is not easy, but it is the only path for those who desire to live eternally in heaven with Jesus Christ.

This Ephesus road was once traveled by throngs of Artemis worshippers.

Section IV

Persecution

Indeed, all who desire to live a godly life in Christ Jesus will be persecuted, while evil people and impostors will go on from bad to worse, deceiving and being deceived. But as for you, continue in what you have learned and have firmly believed, knowing from whom you learned it and how from childhood you have been acquainted with the sacred writings, which are able to make you wise for salvation through faith in Christ Jesus. All Scripture is breathed out by God and profitable for teaching, for reproof, for correction, and for training in righteousness, that the man of God may be competent, equipped for every good work. (2 Tim. 3:12–17)

Fountain in what was ancient Smyrna, the
first faithful church of Revelation.[34]

Jesus said to her, "Everyone who drinks of this water
will be thirsty again, but whoever drinks of the water
that I will give him will never be thirsty again. The
water that I will give him will become in him a spring
of water welling up to eternal life." (John 4:13–14)

---

[34] This fountain in ancient Smyrna, Izmir, Turkey, is today below street level.
Smyrna's potable running water epitomizes the living water of Jesus Christ.

CHAPTER 4
Smyrna—Faithful Endurance

And to the angel of the church in Smyrna write: "The words of the first and the last, who died and came to life.

"I know your tribulation and your poverty (but you are rich) and the slander of those who say that they are Jews and are not, but are a synagogue of Satan. Do not fear what you are about to suffer. Behold, the devil is about to throw some of you into prison, that you may be tested, and for ten days you will have tribulation. Be faithful unto death, and I will give you the crown of life. He who has an ear, let him hear what the Spirit says to the churches. The one who conquers will not be hurt by the second death." (Rev. 2:8–11)

Jesus's message to the Smyrna church is in stark contrast to the letter written to the Ephesian church. Although the church in Ephesus experienced some persecution (such as that of Paul recorded in Acts 19 and Timothy's severe beating and subsequent death in 97 AD), it was not persecuted for its faith as the church in Smyrna was. The Ephesian church was affluent; the Smyrna church was poor. The body of faithful Christians living in Smyrna drank freely of living water. They received no rebuke or consequences from Jesus in their letter, the shortest of the seven letters. Their lampstand would remain because they were faithful.

Paul wrote Timothy, his young co-worker, from prison about thirty years before the book of Revelation was written. He told Timothy that everyone who desired to live a godly life in Jesus would be persecuted, while evil, deceitful people would fall further into deception. Those persecuted for their faith are victorious; those who continue in sin are lost. The Bible provides sufficient knowledge for everyone to know what is of God and be confident in their salvation. The Holy Spirit strengthens Christians to remain faithful.

Where in the World Is Smyrna?

Smyrna lies on the Aegean coast of Turkey in what is the city of Izmir, approximately fifty miles north of Ephesus and sixty-eight miles south of Pergamum. Just off the Mediterranean Sea and sitting on the slope of Mount Pagos (Pagus, under the Roman Empire), Smyrna was a strategically located port city and a major trade route leading inland through Asia Minor. The ruins of the ancient city are surrounded and covered by modern-day Izmir, home to approximately three million people.

The name *Smyrna* may have come from an ancient Greek word for myrrh. Considering the city's rich Greek past, this seems likely. Myrrh is the costly resin of the *Commiphora myrrha* tree that is mixed with other compounds to embalm bodies.[35] It was one of the gifts—gold, frankincense, and myrrh—that the wise men brought to Jesus. Expensive but popular, and a major export of ancient Smyrna, myrrh retards putrefaction.[36] Smyrna is an appropriate name for the persecuted church, especially if one considers the eternal security through salvation in Jesus Christ as spiritual embalming.

---

[35] "Smyrna: The Seven Churches of Revelation," accessed March 13, 2018, http://www.biblestudy.org/biblepic/churches-of-revelation-smyrna.html.
[36] "Smyrna," accessed June 1, 2018, https://en.wikipedia.org/wiki/Smyrna.

History and Archaeology

Originally settled in 3,000 BC or earlier, Smyrna may have been a city of the Leleges (Aegean Aboriginal people) before being resettled by the Greeks in the eleventh century BC. A leading city state of Ionia with great influence in the area, Smyrna was among the cities which claimed Homer as a resident.[37] Smyrna's harbor competed with the harbors of Miletus and Ephesus, but after they silted up, Smyrna was without rival.

Smyrna lost power and prestige after kings of the Mermnad dynasty attacked it, but it regained prominence when Antigonus and Lysimachus under Alexander the Great laid a new city foundation in the late fourth to early third centuries BC. Revitalized, enlarged, and fortified, the acropolis atop Mount Pagos boasted a theater that could seat twenty thousand on its northern slopes, a gymnasium, a stadium, and broad paved roads, many of which were named after temples to Zeus, Cybele, Dionysus, Nemesis, and others. Apollonius of Tyana wrote of the beauty of Smyrna's acropolis. He said that the crown of Smyrna, a familiar phrase that referred to the public buildings that spread out over the city around the slopes of Mount Pagos, resembled a crown on a woman's head.[38]

In 197 BC, after severing its relationship with King Eumenes II of Pergamum, Smyrna looked to the Roman Empire for assistance. With no ties to Rome, Smyrna created Roma, a Roman goddess named for Rome, built a temple to her, making its own cult and showing deep Roman loyalty. The cult became popular throughout the Roman Empire. When Attalid king Attalus III died without an heir in 133 BC, his kingdom was organized into the Roman province of Asia, with Pergamum as its capital. Smyrna became prominent because of its major harbor, which competed with Ephesus and Pergamum to be the first city of Asia.

---

[37] Ibid. Homer is the presumed author of the ancient Greek poems "The Iliad" and "Odyssey."

[38] "Chapter—Smyrna: The City of Life," accessed March 11, 2020, http://www.godrules.net/library/ramsay/44ramsay_a20.htm.

In the first century AD, the population of Smyrna is estimated to have reached one hundred fifty thousand to two hundred thousand inhabitants. Excavations have unearthed twenty-eight shops and businesses all facing north on the ground floor of the agora, the largest marketplace of the ancient world, and a sophisticated system of running water. The second floor contained rows of columns between galleries.

Smyrna had a large wealthy Jewish community. Christianity likely grew out of this Jewish community in the early first century. Because Christianity was considered a subset of Judaism, Christians were exempt from emperor worship, as were the Jews. This changed, as did Jewish treatment of Christians, as the church grew. Early on an archbishopric was established in Smyrna, perhaps one of the few with true apostolic succession, and was promoted to a metropolis in the ninth century. Some believe that Apelles, approved in Christ (Rom. 16:10), was the first bishop of Smyrna. Others believe it was Ariston, succeeded by Strateas, Lois's son and/or Timothy's uncle (2 Tim. 1:5), and then followed by Boucolus.[39] Wikipedia lists the first bishops of Smyrna as Apelles, Strateas (brother or uncle of Timothy), Ariston, Boucolus, and Polycarp.[40]

The early church fathers visited Smyrna and wrote letters to its bishops. Ignatius of Antioch visited Smyrna and wrote Polycarp, Smyrna's most-famous bishop. Tertullian wrote how Smyrna was well equipped to fight heresy, with the sound teachings of Polycarp and John behind them. Irenaeus, Tertullian, and Jerome record that Polycarp was a disciple of John. Irenaeus noted how Polycarp was appointed bishop of Smyrna by apostles in Asia and told of a powerful letter that Polycarp had written to Philippi. Polycarp is regarded as one of three chief apostolic fathers, along with Clement of Rome and Ignatius of Antioch.

The church known for persecution is remembered for the ultimate

---

[39] Otto F. A. Meinardus, "The Christian Remains of the Seven Churches of the Apocalypse," *The Biblical Archaeologist* 37, no. 3 (1974): 69–82.
[40] "Metropolis of Smyrna," accessed October 4, 2020, https://en.wikipedia.org/wiki/Metropolis_of_Smyrna.

sacrifice of its most-famous citizen, Polycarp of Smyrna, but the dates of his death and life are in dispute. According to Eusebius, Polycarp's martyrdom in Smyrna occurred during the reign of Marcus Aurelius, around 167/168. John Foxe dates Polycarp's death during Marcus's fourth persecution, beginning in 162 AD.[41] According to Foxe, Polycarp was bound and burned at the stake after first evading capture. Then discovered by a child, he prayed so fervently with the guards that apprehended him that they repented of taking him. Nevertheless, when fire did not consume him, he was stabbed to death. Told by the proconsul to curse Christ and swear by Lord Caesar, Polycarp replied:

> "For eighty-six years I have been his servant, and he has never done me wrong. How can I blaspheme my King who saved me? … You threaten a fire that burns for a time and is quickly extinguished. Yet a fire you know nothing about awaits the wicked in the judgment to come and in eternal punishment…."
>
> As they were going to nail him to the grid for the fire, he said, "Let me be, for he who enables me to endure the flames will also enable me to remain in them unmoved, even without nails…."
>
> He prayed: "O Father of your beloved Son, Jesus Christ, through whom we know you, I bless you for this day and hour, that I may, with the martyrs, share in the cup of Christ for the resurrection to eternal life of both soul and body in the immortality of the Holy Spirit. May I be received among them today as a rich and acceptable sacrifice, according to your divine fulfillment. For this reason I praise you for everything, I bless and glorify you through the eternal high priest, Jesus Christ, your beloved Son, through whom be glory to you and the Holy Spirit, both now and in the ages to come. Amen."[42]

---

[41] Foxe, *Foxe's Book of Martyrs*, 13.

[42] Paul L. Maier, *Eusebius: The Church History: A New Translation with Commentary* (Grand Rapids, MI: Kregel, 1999), 145–152.

Revelation 2:8

> *And to the angel of the church in Smyrna write: The words of the first and the last, who died and came to life.*

"The words of the first and the last" refer to Jesus's words of Revelation 1:8: "I am the Alpha and the Omega, who is and who was and who is to come, the Almighty." Jesus's teachings clarify that He is the first and the last, the Alpha and the Omega, the beginning and the end. He is, He was, and He is to come, the Almighty.

The words of Revelation 2:8 leave no room for doubt that Jesus is speaking, and He, like the Father, is outside of time and space. The One speaking through John is the Lord Jesus Christ, who died and was resurrected, "the faithful witness, the first born of the dead, and the ruler of kings on earth" (Rev. 1:5). Jesus delivers Christians from sin by His blood so that they do not suffer the second death.

Historically, Smyrna has always been associated with the persecuted Christian church. Persecuted Christians who die for their faith in Jesus have no fear of death or of hell because they will be resurrected to live with Christ forever.

Revelation 2:9

> *I know your tribulation and your poverty (but you are rich) and the slander of those who say that they are Jews and are not but are a synagogue of Satan.*

Jesus tells this church that He knows their troubles. As God, He knows about their poverty and its repercussions that resulted from the slander of the Jews who despised them. They are rich because they know Jesus and are washed in His blood. Members of this church are rich in righteousness. They will not deny Jesus to get ahead in their earthly lives. Jesus knows how the Christians in

Smyrna are treated, how that the Jews are pawns of Satan. Jesus reassures them that eternity with Him is theirs because of their faithful, patient endurance.

Revelation 2:10

> *Do not fear what you are about to suffer. Behold, the devil is about to throw some of you into prison, that you may be tested, and for ten days you will have tribulation.*

This letter must have brought Christians to their knees. They loved each other and must have prayed for one another to be borne up under the coming persecution. They were assured that suffering would be for a specified period but that it would not mean spiritual defeat. Through their faithful and patient endurance, their persecution meant spiritual and eternal victory. The indwelling Holy Spirit strengthened their footsteps. Some would be thrown into prison to be tested for ten days. Here the number *ten* signified the optimal time under divine order.[43] They would endure it. Compared with Jesus's horrific persecution and death, where few lovingly and openly supported Him, their being imprisoned for ten days would be easy. At the time of their letter, Christians in Smyrna had been persecuted but not to the extent that they would later be persecuted.

Revelation 2:11

> *Be faithful unto death, and I will give you the crown of life. He who has an ear, let him hear what the Spirit says to the churches. The one who conquers will not be hurt by the second death.*

---

[43] "The Significance of Numbers in Scripture," Agape Bible Study, accessed July 5, 2018, http://www.agapebiblestudy.com/documents/The%20Significance%20of%20Numbers%20in%20Scripture.htm. In the Bible, some numbers have great significance in addition to their numeric value.

Although Smyrna had schools and a library, it was best known for its cultural activities: drama in the odeon, entertainment in the theater, and competitive sports in the most spectacular gymnasium in Asia Minor. Smyrna was an Olympic city. Its citizens knew about Olympic sports and how each victor received a crown of olive branches. The Olympian games and the acropolis landmark crown of Smyrna added to the city's popularity.

Christians in Smyrna may not have frequented the theater, the stadium, or the gymnasium; most of them were poor, second-class citizens ostracized because of their belief in Jesus as Lord. Because they refused to pay tribute to Roman gods and sprinkle incense in the emperor's name, they were ridiculed by the Jews and persecuted by the Romans. They knew that receiving a "crown of life" meant eternal life, one that surpassed both the meager crown of olive leaves and branches given to winners in the gymnasium and the famous crown of buildings atop the acropolis.

The church in Smyrna knew that they would win the only race that really matters because they were ultimately victorious in Christ. They knew the writings of Jesus's brother, James, written between 49 and 62 AD: "Blessed is the man who remains steadfast under trial, for when he has stood the test he will receive the crown of life, which God has promised to those who love Him" (James 1:12); this verse contains the only other reference to a crown of life, but at least four references to other heavenly crowns are scattered throughout the New Testament.

Putting the Pieces Together

God knew that the church in Smyrna loved Him, whereas the church in Ephesus did not. Ephesus had right teaching, but Smyrna had right teaching and right godly love.

Pagan worship of gods at festivals, prevalent in the Roman Empire, included animal sacrifice. Such festivals broke the commands given to Jews and Christians to worship only God and not to worship idols or make graven images. Ancient Greek Olympic games were rooted in pagan mythology and worship, specifically the worship of Zeus. Byzantine emperor and devout Christian Theodosius I is credited with banning pagan rituals, including the Olympic games and the worship of the oracle of Delphi, in the late fourth century (c.393).[44] He knew the prophets' warnings about false worship that mixes idolatry with vain offerings at feasts and festivals (e.g., Isa. 1:2–31; Mal. 1:6–14).

When Christians compromise their faith in order to live trouble-free lives, they jeopardize their salvation and eternal lives. God's truth holds Christians to the narrow path, the right way of living in the world, which is why early Christians were called the "people of the way." They lived God's truth in love, to Him first, and then to others. First-century Christians believed that Jesus could come at any time.

John taught the Smyrna church that it should be ready, prepared, and awake for Jesus's return at any time (Matt. 24, Mark 13, Luke 21). Because they stood firm for Christ, these Christians lacked job security but worked diligently to feed their families. It would have been difficult for parents to watch their children go hungry when much of Smyrna's population gorged themselves at pagan feasts that they, as Christians, could not and would not attend. The church in Smyrna knew that one day it would be with Jesus in heaven, although it had poor living conditions on earth. Their love for God was of primary importance. Being "Christian" for many today does not mean following the Bible as the first-century Smyrna church did, but those who do follow the one true God of the Bible believe what this church believed.

---

[44] "Theodosius I," accessed May 7, 2020, https://en.wikipwedia.org/w/index.php?title=Theodosius_I&oldid=955303269.

Hatred and Persecution

From its beginning, Christianity was hated and its adherents persecuted. In the first century, persecution was not deemed a crime. Christians expected persecution, and they learned to persevere for the gospel. Even prior to Christ's death, His followers died for their beliefs. John the Baptist was one of the first. Beginning with Stephen, the first martyr, billions have died because of their refusal to renounce their faith in Christ. Paul, who became a pillar of Christianity, was ruthless as Saul the Roman Pharisee who hated and hunted down Christians. One day God called him, and he believed. Then Paul was hated, hunted down, and persecuted, as he himself had done to others. Paul knew much about persecution and wrote about it in his epistles. The church in Smyrna became known for its uncompromising faith during persecution.

More Christians are imprisoned and tortured today than followers of any other religion, sometimes for even carrying a Bible. Christian international human rights non-governmental organizations keeping statistics on persecution document that the persecution of Christians is worsening. Every day Christians lose their freedom, their property, their homes, and their lives for following Christ. Throughout the centuries, thousands of Christians have left home and family to go to far-off lands and spread the gospel, risking their lives to do so. In recent years, missionary work has been criticized because it is said to contribute to the loss of Indigenous culture. Although missionary work continues, it now has a different focus.

Some areas of the world experience harsher persecution than others. Reports of Christians being beheaded because they refused to deny Christ, of large numbers of church worshippers slain together, girls being abducted, and genocide are painful to hear but much more difficult to experience. These martyrs lived and died for Jesus. Their eternity is secure, but some today do not wish to hear or have these stories told.

The Christian population of Turkey is steadily declining. It is easier for Christians to move there for work and practice their faith than for Turkish converts to Christianity to practice theirs. It is easier in some areas of Turkey to be a Christian than in others. Most of the population is Muslim. On April 18, 2007, three Christians were brutally murdered in Zirve Publishing House in Malatya, Western Turkey. Two were Turkish Christians and one a German who was committed to taking the gospel to the Turkish people because God had called him.[45] Five young Muslim men known by their victims charged with the murders may spend the rest of their lives in prison. Although three men were killed that fateful day, hundreds of lives were forever changed. Another account of Christian persecution in Turkey, *God's Hostage,* gives a record of Pastor Andrew Brunson's ministry in Izmir (Smyrna) and his two years in Turkish jails, which forever changed his and his family's lives.[46] Such events discourage some from visiting Turkey, home of all seven of the churches of Revelation.

Missionary work around the world is hampered when anyone's safety is at risk but some bravely discount their own well-being to bring the saving knowledge of Jesus Christ to those who do not have it. This work can happen peacefully, but it often brings some level of hatred and persecution. God equips those who love others with His love to spread the gospel despite the tension, strife, and threat of loss of property or life.

Smyrna in Our Time

Even though many of those persecuted today know that they will be eternally rewarded because of their faithfulness, living through persecution is difficult. The few Christians living in Turkey know that they live under the real threat of persecution. All Christians who live

---

[45] James Wright, *The Martyrs of Malatya: Martyred for the Messiah in Turkey* (Grand Rapids, MI: EP Books, 2015).

[46] Andrew Brunson with Craig Borlase, *God's Hostage: A True Story of Persecution, Imprisonment, and Perseverance* (Grand Rapids, MI: Baker Books, 2019).

in unsafe areas risk their lives because they know that eternal life for non-Christians is more important than their own mortal lives.

Christians all over the world are hated and persecuted for believing in Jesus as the Son of God. Many of them live with constant threats of physical harm to the point of death. Jesus's message to Smyrna is as pertinent to twenty-first century Christians as it was for those of the first century. It speaks to everyone who is being or will be persecuted because of their love for God.

The world is not the happy place that those living an easy and abundant life think and promote it to be. A spiritual war rages. All the while God's love and goodness shines through the Holy Spirit in Christians, who, with God's angels, wrestle the evil of the devil and his army. The primary questions that everyone must ask themselves, sooner rather than later, are, "Whose side am I on?" and "Do I worship and serve God, or do I not?" Everyone will answer one day.

The persecuted are not consumed with accumulating earthly treasure; they know that all material possessions will be lost, stolen, or decay. Christians have a firm foundation that will never be lost, stolen, or decay. Wise people surround themselves with heavenly treasures, as Jesus taught:

> Do not lay up for yourselves treasures on earth, where moth and rust destroy and where thieves break in and steal, but lay up for yourselves treasures in heaven, where neither moth nor rust destroys and where thieves do not break in and steal. For where your treasure is, there your heart will be also. (Matt. 6:19–21)

Persecution for Christ

Revelation reveals how life as we know it will culminate with the return of Christ. Present-day Christians have nothing to fear when this happens, but what many of them face every day would make many people cower. Those who love the Lord fear losing Him, not their possessions or their lives. Many who are persecuted do not want their persecution removed but want the strength to endure the persecution for the glory of God. They desire prayers, not financial support. The Bible encourages and comforts the persecuted and those living in threat of persecution: a loving omnipotent God gives them what no person, family, community, or government ever can.

Every year Open Doors World Watch List reports the top fifty countries in which Christians suffer the most persecution. According to the 2020 report, eight Christians every day are killed for their faith in Jesus, 182 churches or Christian buildings every week are attacked, and 309 Christians every month are imprisoned for no valid reason. The 2021 World Watch List reports even greater numbers, with approximately one in eight Christians worldwide persecuted because of their faith.[47]

The Fellowship of the Unashamed

The following poem, "The Fellowship of the Unashamed," on the internet for several years in varying versions, lists the author as unknown. Most say that he was an African pastor, possibly from Zimbabwe or Rwanda, who died for his faith forty to one hundred-plus years ago. The poem, found among his personal possessions after he was martyred, is a tribute to his faith and character.

> I am part of the fellowship of the unashamed. I have Holy Spirit power.
> The die has been cast. I have stepped over the line. The decision has been made. I am a disciple of his. I won't look back, let up, slow down, back away or be still.

---

[47] "The Top 50 Countries Where It's Hardest to Be a Christian," *Christianity Today,* posted January 15, 2020, accessed March 6, 2020, https://www.christianitytoday. com/news/2020/january/top-christian-persecution-open-doors-2020-world-watch-list.html. See also "2021 World Watch List: The 50 Most Dangerous Countries to Be a Christian." This source reported that COVID-19 was yet another tool used to discriminate against Christians.

My past is redeemed. My present makes sense. My future is secure. I'm finished with low living, sight walking, small planning, smooth knees, colorless dreams, tamed visions, worldly talking, cheap giving, and dwarfed goals.

I no longer need prominence, prosperity, position, promotions, plaudits, or popularity. I don't have to be right, first, tops, recognized, praised, regarded or rewarded. I now live by faith, lean on his presence, walk by patience, am lifted by prayer and labor by power.

My pace is set. My gait is fast. My goal is heaven. My road is narrow. My way rough. My companions few. My guide is reliable and my mission is clear.

I cannot be bought, compromised, detoured, lured away, turned back, deluded or delayed.

I will not flinch in the face of sacrifice, hesitate in the presence of the adversary, negotiate at the table of the enemy, ponder at the pool of popularity or meander in the maze of mediocrity.

I won't give up, shut up, let up, until I've stayed up, stored up, prayed up, paid up, preached up for the cause of Christ.

I am a disciple of Jesus. I must go till he comes, give till I drop, preach till all know, and work till he stops me. And when he comes for his own, he'll have no problem recognizing me. My banner will be clear![48]

This author gave up all that he knew that he would lose to gain all that he knew that he would keep forever. Whoever he was, he followed Jesus and did not turn back. Sure of his identity in Christ, he knew that Jesus would recognize him as His brother when He returns for His church. This anonymous author left a lasting and visible legacy of encouragement for the whole church.

---

[48] This version is a compilation of several versions, including "What Is The Fellowship of the Unashamed?" Reasons for Hope Jesus, accessed April 3, 2020, https://reasonsforhopejesus.com/what-is-the-fellowship-of-the-unashamed/ and "The Fellowship of the Unashamed," Precept Ministries International, accessed April 3, 2020, https://www.precept.org/2014/07/13/the-fellowship-of-the-unashamed.

We cannot go far without seeing pain. If we visit the sick in hospital, the infirm and the elderly in acute-care facilities, the grieving in funeral homes, or those in prison, pain and suffering are evident. Some in prison speak of psychological, emotional, and spiritual pain in addition to their physical pain, but many report that their spiritual pain is the most difficult to endure. Pain for all Christians will end when Jesus returns but, according to the Bible, this is the beginning of pain for non-Christians.

John knew suffering but wrote expectantly of the true joy and hope of Jesus in his epistles. Paul and most of the twelve apostles endured horrendous deaths, as did many early Christians. But no one was persecuted, or ever will be, to the extent that Jesus was. He bore His pain, humiliation, and heartache out of love for us. Revelation foretells further suffering before Jesus returns, but Christians know that their eternal security is secure. The church in Smyrna knew this, as do those persecuted today.

Like most of Jesus's family and most in Nazareth, Jesus's oldest brother, James, called the Just, did not believe that Jesus was who He said He was while Jesus was alive. Like Jesus's family, some in Nazareth, some Pharisees, scribes, and Jewish leaders, James came to believe that Jesus was God after His death and resurrection. James, the first bishop of Jerusalem, was martyred for his faith around 62 or 69 AD.

God sometimes chooses the poorest financially who love Him with their whole hearts to be the richest in faith and inherit His kingdom. The blood of the martyrs is the seed of the church, as Polycarp of Smyrna, Jesus's brother James, and modern-day Turkish martyrs exemplify. James wrote, "Listen, my beloved brothers, has not God chosen those who are poor in the world to be rich in faith and heirs of the kingdom, which he has promised to those who love him?" (James 2:5). Yes, God chooses some of the poor to lead the way, but not all the poor will be saved, just as not all the rich will be lost.

Although the Christian road is narrow, it is possible for the rich to know Jesus, love him, and follow him, through accepting

Him and obeying God. The rich are assured that even the richest may follow Christ and be saved, as were Joseph of Arimathea, Cornelius, the unnamed Roman centurion, Lydia of Thyatira, Nicodemus, Philemon, Zacchaeus, and the wealthy men and women instrumental in early church growth. It is the love of money and what is done with money that is sinful. Regardless of financial worth, everyone can be wise by knowing the Bible and being "quick to hear and slow to speak" (James 1:19). While the poor may find it easier to believe, the rich also find faith in Jesus and work for His Kingdom, knowing that everything has consequences.

The Smyrna letter was written to encourage one specific persecuted church. Its members knew Jesus and were equipped to endure all that would come. This church was a source of encouragement in the first century and still is nineteen hundred years later because it proved that it was possible to be hated and persecuted in the world yet be righteous before God and ensured of eternity in heaven. This letter will provide encouragement to persecuted Christians until Jesus returns. It will also remind those who love God and follow Jesus that, despite their wealth, they too can pass through the narrow gate.

Every person who knows the love of God and the release of their burdens of sin is free as the wealthiest, most powerful non-Christian cannot be. Christians are peace- and joy-filled, rich in grace and mercy, although they may be persecuted for their faith. Overcomers lovingly keep God's commandments to the best of their ability, "for this is the love of God, that we keep His commandments. And His commandments are not burdensome. For everyone who has been born of God overcomes the world. And this is the victory that has overcome the world—our faith" (1 John 5:3–4).

The Bible teaches why the world hates. Jesus tells us to love our enemies because He knows how God's love changes us. He compares thoughts of hatred to murder (Matt. 5:21–22; 1 John 3:15). Many fail to know God and understand His ways because they do not know about Him, or reject Him. Smyrna's Christians knew why the world is evil. They heard, understood, and loved God although their lives were difficult.

Some believe that the persecution of Christians is just beginning, that the years ahead will be more difficult. Jesus's revelation to John encourages Christians to keep the faith, while counting as joy everything they do in Jesus's name.

> Count it all joy, my brothers, when you meet trials of various kinds, for you know that the testing of your faith produces steadfastness. And let steadfastness have its full effect, that you may be perfect and complete, lacking in nothing. (James 1:2–4)

The ancient ruins of Smyrna surrounded by a modern city.

I tell you, my friends, do not fear those who kill the body, and after that have nothing more that they can do. But I will warn you whom to fear: fear him who, after he has killed, has authority to cast into hell. Yes, I tell you, fear him! (Luke 12:4–5)

Underground ruins in Izmir, Turkey, once ancient Smyrna.

Section V

Fighting God

Then Jesus was led by the Spirit into the wilderness to be tempted by the devil. After fasting forty days and forty nights, he was hungry. The tempter came to him and said, "If you are the Son of God, tell these stones to become bread."

Jesus answered, "It is written: 'Man shall not live on bread alone, but on every word that comes from the mouth of God.'"

Then the devil took him to the holy city and had him stand on the highest point of the temple. "If you are the Son of God," he said, "throw yourself down. For it is written:

"'He will command his angels concerning you, and they will lift you up in their hands, so that you will not strike your foot against a stone.'"

Jesus answered him, "It is also written: 'Do not put the Lord your God to the test.'"

Again, the devil took him to a very high mountain and showed him all the kingdoms of the world and their splendor. "All this I will give you," he said, "if you will bow down and worship me."

Jesus said to him, "Away from me, Satan! For it is written: 'Worship the Lord your God, and serve him only.'"

Then the devil left him, and angels came and attended him. (Matt. 4:1–11 NIV)

The LORD said to Cain, "Why are you angry, and why has your face fallen? If you do well, will you not be accepted? And if you do not do well, sin is crouching at the door. Its desire is for you, but you must rule over it." (Gen. 4:6–7)

Archways on Pergamum's acropolis.

CHAPTER 5

Pergamum—Tolerating Sin—of the Devil

And to the angel of the church in Pergamum write: "The words of him who has the sharp two-edged sword.

"I know where you dwell, where Satan's throne is. Yet you hold fast my name, and you did not deny my faith even in the days of Antipas my faithful witness, who was killed among you, where Satan dwells. But I have a few things against you: you have some there who hold the teaching of Balaam, who taught Balak to put a stumbling block before the sons of Israel, so that they might eat food sacrificed to idols and practice sexual immorality. So also you have some who hold the teaching of the Nicolaitans. Therefore repent. If not, I will come to you soon and war against them with the sword of my mouth. He who has an ear, let him hear what the Spirit says to the churches. To the one who conquers I will give some of the hidden manna, and I will give him a white stone, with a new name written on the stone that no one knows except the one who receives it." (Rev. 2:12–17)

At its high point, Pergamum was considered a royal city, but Jesus did not speak highly of it or the church within it. Pergamum was the center of much that was evil and sinful in the first century.

Christians know that they must fight the devil. Tolerating evil and sin in the church and not teaching about God, His ways, and His expectations for His people is the beginning of a slippery slope—one leading away from God and heaven.

Of the Devil, of the Flesh, and of the World

Sin, sometimes classified as being of the world, of the flesh, and of the devil, is an enemy of the soul that can kill a person's relationship and eternal life with God. Sinning usually follows a downward spiral from toleration, to acceptance, and to promotion of that which contravenes God's laws.

Matthew 4 and Luke 4 describe Jesus's temptation in the desert. When the devil tempted Jesus, he first tempted His flesh. If Jesus had turned stones into bread, His hunger would have been satisfied, but He, quoting Deuteronomy 8:3, knew that spiritual food was more important. The devil next tempted Jesus to throw Himself off the temple, which would have made worldly trials unnecessary. Again, Jesus resisted, knowing that He would suffer to save fallen humanity. The devil finally offered Jesus everything if He would but worship him: Jesus worshipped only His Father. In His humanity, Jesus was tempted but did not capitulate to His flesh, the world, or the devil.

This chapter explores the first of sin's threefold path, tolerance, as the crafty hand of the devil. Sin of the flesh and accepting sin because it feels good is the focus of chapter 6. Sin of the world and promoting that which is against God is the focus of chapter 7. The devil is the enemy of all who love, worship, and obey God (Rev. 12:17) because he wants to be God (Isa. 14:12–15; Ezek. 28:13–19). Sin entered the world through Satan, but not all sin comes directly from him.

Where in the World Is Pergamum?

The third church, referred to as Pergamum, Pergamon, and Pergamos, is sixty-eight miles north of Smyrna/Izmir and fifty-two miles northwest of Thyatira. Two miles north of the Caicus River and sixteen miles inland of the Aegean Sea, Pergamum was built on a precipice about 1,165 feet above sea level. The city was joined by road to Thyatira, which continued to Sardis.

The ruins of ancient Pergamum are located within and partially covered by modern-day Bergama city (population approximately seventy thousand) in Bergama district, in the province of Izmir in western Turkey. The archaeological site, a UNESCO World Heritage Site since 2014, is situated northeast of the city center on the acropolis. It may be accessed by foot, by car, or by the Bergama Acropolis cable car. The site is more easily reached by a cable car, which is often out of service on windy days. That leaves the visitor no choice but to walk or drive the long winding road uphill. With high winds and the sun shrouded by cloud, Pergamum is a dark, foreboding place.

History and Archaeology

A small Pergamum settlement existed in antiquity, but little is known of its history. The name was possibly derived from a Hittite word meaning *high settlement*.[49] By the fifth century BC, coins were issued there. In the Hellenistic period, the city became prominent, as the successor to Alexander the Great, Lysimachus, deposited nine thousand talents of gold for war expenses with a regional general, Philetaerus. Upon Lysimachus's death, Philetaerus used the gold to set up his own kingdom, the Attalid Kingdom. The dynasty extended from 282 to 133 BC, with Pergamum as its capital. Pergamum served as a sanctuary for the kings, where they were worshipped as gods.[50] As a religious center of Izmir, it also hosted temples dedicated to

---

[49] "Bergama," accessed May 9, 2019, https://en.wikipedia.org/wiki/Bergama.
[50] "Biblical Sites in Turkey: Pergamum," accessed June 1, 2018, http://www.meandertravel.com/biblical_asia_minor/biblical_asia_minor.php?details=pergamum&m=5&md=sc5.

Zeus, Dionysus, Athena, and Asclepius (or Asklepios),[51] as well as Augustus and the goddess Roma.[52]

Much of Pergamum's acropolis was built by Eumenes II (197–159 BC). He completed most of the work on five city palaces, five theaters, a library, and a 2,700-foot Corinthian colonnade called the Sacred Way, which led to one of the largest medical centers of its day, which was two miles south of the acropolis, in the valley. Built possibly in the fourth century BC, the Asclepion, named for Asclepius, the ancestral god of salvation, medicine, and healing, was also a sanctuary and place of worship.

Eumenes also built an altar to Zeus to commemorate the expansion of the kingdom and victories over the Macedonians, Galatians, and Seleucids during his reign. Meanwhile, at a similar time (c.167–161 BC), Seleucid king Antiochus IV Epiphanes tried to hellenize the Jews; his ordering of worship of the Greek god Zeus in their temple in Jerusalem precipitated the Maccabean Revolt (2 Macc. 6:1–12 NRSV).

In the Roman period, Pergamum, capital of Asia before Ephesus, vied with both Ephesus and Smyrna as the most influential city of the Roman Empire. As the first to align with Rome, Pergamum was the focal point for the worship of Roman emperors. Augustus established it as a place of emperor worship, authorizing the erection of the first temple to Roman emperor Julius Caesar in Asia Minor in 29 BC. In 113/4 AD, Trajan established a second place of emperor worship. In 123 AD, Hadrian ranked Pergamum as a metropolis, elevating it over both Smyrna and Ephesus. The fourth temple of the imperial cult to the emperor Trajan initiated by Trajan himself and finished by Hadrian is one of the most striking features on Pergamum's upper acropolis today. Later a temple was erected to honor Caracalla. Emperor Domitian used these temples to test civic loyalty to the worship of pagan gods and Roman emperors.

According to the writings of Plutarch, Pergamum had the second

---

[51] "Pergamos; Pergamum," accessed September 19, 2020, https://www.internationalstandardbible.com/P/pergamos-pergamum.html.
[52] *ESV Study Bible*, note for Revelation 2:13.

largest library in the ancient Greek world (after Alexandria), with two hundred thousand volumes, built during the reign of Eumenes II. Pergaminus or parchment made of calfskin, which replaced papyrus, was derived from the city's name. Most of the volumes sent to Alexandria when Marc Anthony gave them to Cleopatra as a wedding gift around 40 BC were destroyed by fire.

Health, healing, and medicine at the Asclepion were central to Pergamum daily life. Alternative medicine combined physical, psychological, and spiritual healing through diagnoses that at times included supernatural visits by Asclepius or his daughters. Those that were known to be palliative, or near death, were not permitted to enter the facilities, as only life was spoken of there.[53] Treatments included sleep, water, mud baths by a sacred stream, music therapy, dream analysis, and the administration of highly diluted poisons. Supernatural dogs were sometimes included in the therapy. It was believed that healing came through the worship and handling of snakes and other reptiles. The serpent, an emblem of Asclepius, eventually became the logo of modern medicine.[54] A Pergamene coin depicts Emperor Caracalla with a spear in his hand in front of a snake encircling a staff.

Greek, Egyptian, and Roman gods[55] were all worshipped in Pergamum, but Zeus had special status, as he was called savior. Zeus's altar, build by Eumenes II, also called the Pergamum altar, and Satan's throne in Revelation, was a focal point of the city. Its striking pagan scenes on friezes, with the gods of Olympus represented as giants with serpent-like tails, were (and still are) extremely popular.

The great temple of the Egyptian god Isis or Serapis, called the Red Basilica, had courtyards with pools at each end for ablutions. The main building of the Red Basilica likely housed the church of

---

[53] "The Seat of Satan: Ancient Pergamum," accessed May 9, 2019, www1.cbn.com /700 club/seat-satan-ancient-pergamum.

[54] The most-famous physician in the ancient Roman Empire, Galen, born in Pergamum in 129 AD, served emperors Marcus Aurelius, Commodus, and Septimius Severus. He trained and worked at Pergamum's Asclepion.

[55] Including Osiris, Serapis, Harpocrates, Zeus, Hera, Demeter, Asclepius, Athena, and Trajan.

Revelation.[56] The Byzantines erected a church over the site in the second century AD. The forecourt of the Red Basilica, supported today by the 633-foot-long Pergamum Bridge, is the largest bridge substructure of antiquity.[57]

Pergamum's population grew to approximately two hundred thousand before its economy collapsed, and the city declined after an earthquake in 262 AD.[58] The base of the Altar of Zeus remains in Pergamum but most of Satan's throne, including the friezes, are among the famous items of the Berlin Collection of Classical Antiquities on display in the Pergamon and Altes Museums on Berlin Museum Island, which was built to house the Pergamum antiquities that were moved there by archaeologists in the late nineteenth century.

Inwardly Digesting Revelation 2:12–17

The church in Pergamum, situated in a culturally rich and politically powerful environment, was influenced by false teaching just as Ephesus was and experienced persecution just as Smyrna did. The place where Satan dwelled was littered with every imaginable sin. It would have been impossible to avoid seeing or being influenced by pagan worship, hedonism, and every sort of medical and alternative intervention that could be devised to heal, seduce, cure, and pleasure the body physically, emotionally, and spiritually. There was rampant sexual perversion, especially during pagan worship. Human sacrifices were also associated with Satan's throne, the Altar of Zeus.

---

[56] "Pergamon," accessed January 4, 2020, www.turkishculture.org/archaeology/Pergamum-1020.htm.
[57] "Pergamon," accessed June 1, 2018, https://en.wikipedia.org/wiki/Pergamon.
[58] Ibid.

Ruins of the temple to Trajan, atop the acropolis, Pergamum, Turkey.

Revelation 2:12–13

And to the angel of the church in Pergamum write:
The words of him who has the sharp two-edged
sword.
I know where you dwell, where Satan's throne is.
Yet you hold fast my name, and you did not deny my
faith even in the days of Antipas, my faithful witness,
who was killed among you, where Satan dwells.

The church in Pergamum would have been familiar with a huge sword much like a gigantic ulu held out with both arms and swung back and forth during battle to butcher large numbers of people at one time. They would have known of the gruesome fates of many of their kinsmen, especially of the martyrdom of a bishop a few years before they received their letter. They also knew that this was not Jesus's sword.

This church at one time had faithful teaching. It knew Jesus as the One with the sharp two-edged sword and would have been familiar with Hebrews 4:12, written decades earlier: "For the word of God is living and active, sharper than any two-edged sword, piercing to the division of soul and spirit, of joints and of marrow, and discerning the thoughts and intentions of heart."

God's Word separates those who are His from those who are not. Antipas, and possibly others in Pergamum, kept the faith. We can only imagine how the hearts of the faithful overflowed as they heard John's letter being read. Jesus knew that the church in Pergamum was in dire straits, because He knew where Satan dwelled and all that went on there. He praised the church for its steadfastness. Even as Antipas perished in a hollow brazen bull, crying out in prayer for them as he was being martyred, some remained faithful. Christians would have prayed for strength and protection to endure living amid the cult of Asclepius in snake-infested temples. Only God and His angels could have equipped Christians to endure life in such a reptile-loving pagan, Greek, Egyptian, and Roman society and to withstand the ensuing persecution.

Antipas, ordained Pergamum's first bishop by the apostle John, and John are the only two Christians named by Jesus in the seven letters. Antipas was a victim of a clash between pagan worshippers and Christians after he cast out demons one day. An angry mob burned him alive inside a hollow bronze bull in 92 AD. In this gruesome method, a victim was bound and put inside the bull through a side door in such a way that his head lay inside the bull's head. As Antipas was roasted to death by fires underneath him, Christians prayed for him, probably silently, as the pipes inside the bull's head reverberated his death moans, much to the delight of the ferocious crowd below.[59]

Living where the devil had his dwelling place must have been horrendous for those Christians. Some can discern when a place is dark and evil; others, oblivious to evil, feel comfortable, even at home, in such an environment. Living in the devil's lair can be compared to frogs being boiled to death gently in a pot. Because the change in water temperature is so gradual, they do not jump out. Similarly, some people gradually became acclimatized to the evil all around them.

Revelation 2:14–16

> But I have a few things against you; you have some there who hold the teaching of Balaam, who taught Balak to put a stumbling block before the sons of Israel, so that they might eat food sacrificed to idols and practice sexual immorality. So also you have some who hold the teaching of the Nicolaitans. Therefore repent. If not, I will come to you soon and war against them with the sword of my mouth.

Although Jesus praised the Pergamum church for not denying Him, He knew that some were being tempted by Satan, followed the sinful ways of Balaam, and compromised their faith like the

---

[59] "The Seat of Satan: Pergamum and Nazi Germany," July 22, 2011, accessed April 1, 2020, https://www.youtube.com/watch?reload=9&v=9r83Z Rissyw&list=PLItZgKNA350zIMICTFAk0PAm_7jDI0mqC&index=56&t=0s.

Nicolaitans did. He warned the church that by tolerating evil teachings, eating food offered to idols, being sexually immoral, and practicing divination and witchcraft, some are lost. Jesus taught how sin destroys people's love for God when evil things are first tolerated in their church, and then some participate in that which Jesus detests. Christians in Pergamum were in peril because of this. Satan was vying for their attention and rejoicing in their sins. God knew the strength of Satan's hold.

Christians knew that they should have nothing to do with the devil or with any sin. Those who were committing sins knew that they must repent or be lost. We do not know how long they had to repent, but we do know that Jesus said that He would come suddenly. There would be little warning and no time to repent when Jesus came to fight Pergamum's sin with His double-edged sword. The Bible, too, is double-edged—it teaches truth—separating Christians from non-Christians. It is loved by Christians but perilous to non-Christians. When Jesus comes again with His double-edged sword, the unrepentant will be separated from God forever.

Revelation 2:17

> He who has an ear, let him hear what the Spirit says to the churches. To the one who conquers I will give some of the hidden manna, and I will give him a white stone, with a new name written on the stone that no one knows except the one who receives it.

Christians cannot serve two masters (Matt. 6:24). Some in the Pergamum church were faithful, but those who tried to appease the rulers by tolerating the teachings of Balaam and the Nicolaitans were not faithful to God. It is a sin to compromise on wrong doctrine while following Jesus. Each person had to choose between serving Balaam and/or the Nicolaitans, pleasing Rome and Satan or being faithful to God. Jesus taught that they must not eat food sacrificed to idols, commit sexual sin, or worship anything or anyone except God. The choice: repent or be lost forever.

To the victors would be given hidden manna. The word *manna* refers to the food God provided which sustained the Israelites during their sojourn in the desert. Here in Revelation Jesus is referring to spiritual food that would strengthen Christians to live faithfully in a spiritually dark world. This hidden manna could have been Scripture, God's Word, which Christians would have taken to heart and memorized.

The white stones with new names written on them that no one would understand except those receiving them refers to the new status found through faith in Christ. No longer are souls black or sinful, but they are white, acquitted by Jesus Himself. Christ's church has always had hidden Christians who have been kept safe by the Holy Spirit and who kept their faith secret. Known only by God and the few faithful protecting them and with whom they congregate, these faithful are fed with spiritual manna, enduring whatever they must suffer. Mysteriously, sometimes God protects His people by placing non-Christians in a stupor so that they are unable to see, hear, or understand. Because of the love of their heavenly Father, Christians are enabled to withstand persecution.

Putting the Pieces Together

Jesus said that Satan dwelled in Pergamum, the religious center of Asia Minor. Home to the imperial cult, emperor worship was as prevalent there as was worship of pagan gods. Zeus's altar or throne, Satan's dwelling place, was surrounded by snake friezes that were popular in the temple to Asclepius and at the Asclepion. The citizens of Pergamum held to the teachings of Balaam and the Nicolaitans. Satan's presence was palpable, as his demons roamed about, freely seeking whom they might devour. Pagan and emperor worship, and Asclepions offering hope of physical wellness, were popular throughout the area. Both had infiltrated many cultures, as did the teachings of Balaam and the Nicolaitans, but there was only one altar of Zeus. All seven churches were threatened by Satan, and, although only five were under his direct influence, none was as dark as Pergamum.

At the end of the eighteenth century, Satan's throne was moved to Berlin, Germany. Chief Nazi party architect Albert Speer used it as the template for the site of the yearly Nazi parade grounds and rallies in Nuremberg. A podium for Adolf Hitler to address the nation was erected where the hollow brazen bull used to martyr Antipas in Pergamum once stood. The Germans were captivated by Hitler. What happened within three years of Satan's throne's reassembly and the reconstruction of the Ishtar Gate of Babylon in the Pergamon Museum in Berlin in 1930 changed the course of history.

Hitler borrowed heavily from the church to create a worshipful atmosphere for his speeches and ceremonies. "The concluding meeting in Nuremberg must be exactly as solemnly and ceremonially performed as a service of the Catholic Church," he stated. Popular nighttime propaganda meetings attended by hundreds of thousands were transformed by a spectacular cathedral of one hundred fifty searchlights which built a frenzy of German patriotism for Hitler, who loved to be worshipped. After his admirers devotedly sang "Hail Hitler to Thee," Hitler mesmerized them with his fanaticism. *Triumph of the Will*, released in 1934 and broadcast for twelve years, was the only film made about Hitler. It portrayed him as a god.

The September 15, 1936, Nuremberg laws led to the marginalization, torture, imprisonment, and eventual death of over six million Jews. Hitler incited millions to hate and exterminate almost an entire race. The word *holocaust* comes from the Greek word *holokauston*, meaning "a wholly burnt sacrifice."[60] Hitler's desire to build the perfect Aryan race by exterminating specific groups, including Jews and the disabled, through eugenics, showcased

---

[60] Gordon Robertson, "The Seat of Satan: Ancient Pergamum," accessed May 9, 2019, www1.cbn.com/700club/seat-satan-ancient-pergamum, and "The Seat of Satan: Nazi Germany," accessed January 4, 2020, https://www1.cbn.com>seat-satan-nazi-germany.

the worst in humanity. Eugenics, whether considered science or pseudoscience, is evil. It is related to scientific or biological racism evident in Europe since at least the early nineteenth century and it is still being practiced today.

Tolerating Sin: Of the Devil

God created the devil as an angel of light before He created the world. The devil had, and still has, miniscule power compared to that of the Father, Son, or Holy Spirit, the three persons of the uncreated Godhead. Discontented with not being first, and wanting to be God Himself, the devil plotted against God and deceived people into following him. Some see the monumental war between good and evil that is described in the Bible as mythological and scientifically unreasonable. But Christians understand it to be absolute truth, of God, yet unsure of how it is so. Sin crouches at the door of every human heart, waiting to be let inside. All are tempted as Jesus was, but Jesus did not sin.

The Father of Lies

Satan said to Eve, "You will not surely die. For God knows that when you eat of the fruit your eyes will be opened, and you will be like God, knowing good and evil" (Gen. 3:4). Eve ate the fruit and gave it to Adam, who also ate. As their eyes were opened to their nakedness, they made loincloths out of *fig* leaves, the second biblical species which represents Israel.[61] Ever since, men and women have blamed the other for their sins. Sweet figs of a tree that represent Israel are bittersweet for Jews, as they are a constant reminder of their first sin and expulsion from the garden of Eden.

The devil is crafty and a malicious liar. In his biblical debut as a talking serpent, he convinces Eve to partake of the fruit of the tree of good and evil. We know that this snake is the devil because of hints

---

[61] See n.14.

throughout the Bible, but we are sure of his identity by the time we study Revelation. Revelation 12:9 and 20:2 reveal the dragon to be that ancient serpent who is called the devil, Satan, and the father of lies (John 8:44).

Since the fall of humanity, people have rebelled against God's goodness and grown closer to the devil's evil. Earthquakes, floods, famines, hurricanes, and wars increase and intensify as the world moves even further from God. Birth defects, infertility, and new, more virulent diseases appear. Hatred, crime, violence, and perversion escalate. God knows why these things happen. Revelation warns of them.

Eve surely did die. Adam too. They were expelled from the garden, separated from God, as have all subsequent humans. Unless they are in Jesus, no one survives the second death, because they have sinned against God. Anger, greed, gluttony, sloth, lust, envy, and pride constitute the seven deadly sins, but pride is the worst.

Pride: Satan's Fall from Glory

Why is pride considered the worst sin and the root of all evil? It is often equated with self-esteem and important to self-respect, both of which are regarded as positive personal attributes. A certain amount and type of pride is good, but when it is arrogant and haughty, pride is sinful and may precede a fall. It is appropriate to feel good about one's health and countenance, but to feel better than others, and in Satan's case, to feel beautiful enough to replace God, destroys spiritual health. We may never know why Satan fell from God's grace, taking about a third of the angels with him, but he did. He wants to be worshipped as God. While he still rules planet earth, he will tempt as many as he can to accompany him. Hitler followed Satan and was successful in enticing many to follow him: few refused to raise their right arm in allegiance.

Some languages have more than one word for pride, and therefore it is easier to separate appropriate pride from sinful pride. The pride that is the worst of the deadly sins is best referred to as *hubris*, or excessive pride. In a world that understands little to be sinful, hubris is not considered wrong. Christians must understand God's warning against pride, if they are to fight it; to God, a prideful heart is sinful.

Satan fell from glory because of his pride. His beauty made him proud, and he corrupted his wisdom for the sake of his splendor (Ezek. 28:17). Beauty is always desirous, and sometimes worshipped: in nature, in art, and especially in the physical body. Hellenistic society, in particular, highly regarded the human physique. Some people spend too much time and resources on seeking the perfect form. The Bible warns that "charm is deceitful, and beauty is vain, but a woman [and a man] who fears the LORD is to be praised" (Prov. 31:30). People are wise to remember that it is not beauty that is sinful, but pride.[62]

Pride, even if considered appropriate, may be contentious, because faith in Jesus is often what makes pride a vice. In non-Christian eyes, there is no sin, and therefore pride is not sinful. Christians usually see nothing sinful about it either when people put in hard honest work and take pride of ownership with humility and thankfulness to God. But when accomplishments are treated with an arrogance that says, *I did it my way and for myself, and I thank only myself for it*, Christians know that this pride that does not acknowledge that everything comes from God is a vice.

Contemplating Satan may be frightening to some but not to those who know God through His Son and who are indwelled by the Holy Spirit. Job reveals a little about him in Job 41:33–34: "On earth there is not his like, a creature without fear. He sees everything that

---

[62] The Miss USA 2019 beauty pageant was concluding on May 2, 2019, but before the winner received her crown and took her victory walk, the reigning Miss USA 2018, the radiant Sarah Rose Summers, from Nebraska, made her final official appearance and said, "Life is truly amazing. Our God is so good at writing our stories better than I could have ever imagined." Beauty contestants are trained to exude confidence; faith is not encouraged, but now and then some speak of it. Faith is something that may draw some to either support, or withhold support, from others. "Miss USA 2018—Final Walk Sarah Rose Summers," May 4, 2019, accessed July 4, 2020, https://www.youtube.com/watch?v=w96vb4w1wn0.

is high; he is king over all the sons of pride." The prideful heart is especially grievous to God, and the devil specializes in hubris and prideful hearts.

Although Satan has greater power than humans, his power cannot be compared to God's. The devil has been defeated. Faithful, obedient Christians, under God's protection, do not need to fear him. Satan and his demons are fallen creatures. Their end is assured. None of them is omnipotent, omniscient, or omnipresent. The devil and his army are to be respected but not revered. We must not credit them with more than God permits them to do. But we must guard against them and against a prideful heart.

Pergamum in Our Time

> Jesus said to them, "If God were your Father, you would love me, for I came from God and I am here. I came not of my own accord, but he sent me. Why do you not understand what I say? It is because you cannot bear to hear my word. You are of your father the devil, and your will is to do your father's desires. He was a murderer from the beginning, and has nothing to do with the truth, because there is no truth in him. When he lies, he speaks out of his own character, for he is a liar and the father of lies." (John 8:42–44)

Jesus's words in John 8 are alarming to those who see Jesus as a good God compared to what they see as the wrathful, vengeful God of the Old Testament. These same people also see the New Testament as loving and peace-filled, which proves that they have not read or understood the Bible in its entirety. Violence and bloodshed is not what Jesus wages and speaks of when He says, "If anyone comes to me and does not hate his own father and mother and wife and children and brothers and sisters, yes, and even his own life, he cannot be my disciple" (Luke 14:26), but it causes many to squirm. Jesus teaches of the importance of faith in Him over faith in sinful people. Both the Old and New Testaments warn of the war that rages within everyone and tempts them to go against God. Jesus identifies two choices: a person is of God or of the devil. Jesus's words to the Pharisees testing Him should cause readers to think about humanity's inherent nature, whether it is good or evil. Those without understanding cannot bear to hear His words, because their father is not His Father: this is a lethal rebuke. Everyone must beware of evil but not be overwhelmed by the devil.

God created the devil to be beautiful, but he was not satisfied. He wanted more and willingly gave up his heritage as an angel of God. He delights in stealing Christians' heritage as God's children, which is easier when they do not take him and sin seriously. Sin is not taught in many churches; some church leaders do not believe in its existence. When it is used, the term *sin* generally means infractions against established laws of the land, not God's laws. All first-century churches believed in and knew what sin was.

The Bible makes it clear that "whoever makes a practice of sinning is of the devil, for the devil has been sinning from the beginning. The reason Jesus appeared was to destroy the works of the devil" (1 John 3:8). Christ was born to destroy the devil's works and to save humanity. The devil deceives, murders, and destroys, but the Word of God gives life. Later in verse 10, we read, "By this it is evident who are the children of God, and who are the children of the devil: whoever does not practice righteousness is not of God, nor is the one who does not love his brother." John spoke equally of righteousness and love. He knew that true love involved speaking and living God's truth in love. Telling and living a lie cannot be reconciled with righteousness and faith in God. Christians repent of sin and speak truth while acting righteously in love, as difficult and as unpopular as it may be, because they are wary and intolerant of sin.

For many men and women, regardless of age, status, or education, their clothing, hair, and makeup are as important, if not more so, as the events they attend, for some even more important than Jesus and the Bible. Virtual images and social media make the visual more important than eloquence, social presence, or content validity. Staging and airbrushing make it easier to look attractive for a global audience. Too often, too many people are obsessed with their looks and their clothes. When we want to please and impress ourselves and other people, God, who sees everything wherever we are (Prov. 5:21), is not the first we want to please. Jesus tells us:

> Therefore I tell you, do not be anxious about your life, what you will eat or what you will drink, nor about your body, what you will put on. Is not life more than food, and the body more than clothing? Look at the birds of the air: they neither sow nor reap nor gather into barns, and yet your heavenly Father feeds them. Are you not of more value than they? And which of you by being anxious can add a single hour to the span of life? And why are you anxious about clothing? Consider the lilies of the field, how they grow old and they neither toil nor spin, yet I tell you, even Solomon in all his glory was not arrayed like one of these. But if God so clothes the grass of the field, which today is alive and tomorrow is thrown into the oven, will he not much more clothe you, O you of little faith? Therefore do not be anxious, saying, "What shall we eat" or "What shall we drink?" or "What—shall we wear?" For the Gentiles seek after all these things, and your heavenly Father knows that you need them all. But seek first the kingdom of God and his righteousness, and all these things will be added to you. (Matt. 6:25–33)

The Bible clearly warns against undue concern over appearance. The devil's hubristic fall from glory because of his beauty warns us against doing as he did. Preoccupation with and pride in our bodies do not glorify God. It is idolatry and it separates people from God. Jesus warns us not to be anxious over what we eat, drink, or wear: God will care for us as He cares for the birds in the sky and the flowers in the fields. We are His children, more valuable to Him than all other creatures. We must concern ourselves first with loving God, the greatest love of all, and the only one to be exalted.[63]

The people of Pergamum would have had to be people-pleasers to flourish in their city. People-pleasers conform to the ways of the popular people they wish to emulate. They wear, do, and say what others deem appropriate. In the formative teenage years, passing off such actions as a phase and insignificant to a bright future may seem inconsequential, but it may not be—we do not know our hour of death. Christians in Pergamum would have been pressured to deny Christ.

Thus, begins the slippery slope. The ruler of the world knows those who are his and he uses everything in his power to deceive and lure others away from God. Paul warned the Colossians that they would always struggle with their flesh and the ways of the world, but if they were Christians "raised with Christ," they must "seek those things which are above, where Christ is, sitting at the right hand of God. Set your mind on things above, not on things on the earth" (Col. 3:1–2). Christians need God's Word and they need to pray to God for strength to persevere.

One positive aspect of crises is that they can help people realize the tentative nature of life. Some may stop, contemplate their mortality and the meaning of life, and realize that they are dancing with the devil and giving him a foothold in their souls. God stirs hearts to want to change. His call helps people to see how sin hurts Him, and them; it cannot be tolerated, much less belittled by phrases like "the devil made me do it." Some use HALT, a tool of addictions therapy and counseling: No one should ever allow themselves to get too hungry, angry, lonely, or tired, because these weaken the ability to resist temptation and make it easier to capitulate to sin.

---

[63] "The haughty looks of men shall be brought low, and the lofty pride of men shall be humbled, and the Lord alone will be exalted in that day" (Isa. 2:11,17). Beauty and pride can be greatly manifested in leaders. Strength of leadership is a valuable quality, but when intentions are ungodly, however, charismatic people easily sway the gullible into going where they should not go and doing what they should not do—as the devil does. Satan tempts everyone to follow popular people whom he craftily uses to steal people's souls. Christians must scrutinize whom they follow.

The Bible tells us that the devil prowls around like a wild animal seeking prey to devour. We are assured in 1 Peter 5:9 that, if we resist the devil, firm in our faith, after we have suffered a little, the God of all grace will strengthen us to overcome temptation. Christians throughout the world are tempted by the devil to sin, but they have been given the strength to defeat it. When Jesus returns, He will restore and establish them as part of His household forever, along with Antipas, John, the first-century Christians, and all who have suffered and fought to overcome temptation and evil.

The devil tempts with everything in his arsenal, but his greatest appeal is to pride. It defeated him and it defeated Eve when she believed that she would not die. She believed the devil's lies over God's truth. If we continue in sin, believing that sin is inconsequential because God loves us, the devil has deluded us into believing that we can, like him, be ultimately victorious. But he is not, and neither will we.

Jesus teaches us to be humble like Him. The opposite of humility is arrogance, and few like to be described as arrogant. The devil warred with God and Israel, with Jesus and the church, but he is ultimately defeated (Rev. 12). He could never be God—nor can we. Christians, empowered by the Holy Spirit, want to honor and please God. They do their best in all circumstances, for they know that "God so loved the world, that He gave His Son, that whoever believes in Him should not perish but have eternal life" (John 3:16). Whenever they disobey God's commands, they repent and are forgiven.

Pergamum's message from Jesus was difficult to hear but it was no surprise. The Christians there knew who ruled them. Some clung to faith overcoming and finding the hidden manna that led to new names on white stones (eternal life), but many did not. They tolerated the sin in their midst which cost them dearly, as it costs many in our day.

The devil knows that his time is short. He looks attractive, even magical, to his prey, as many are easily fooled into following him. Christians must be wary, for even the elect may be deceived. Sin must not be tolerated in a church, because toleration is the beginning of a steep, slippery slope toward acceptance. After acceptance, sin is promoted because it feels good and everyone tolerates, accepts, and participates in it. Sinners choose to and they want everyone else to follow their example, even to death.

In contrast, Christians are reassured that through Jesus they are not going where the devil is going. Hell was created for the devil, his demons, and those following them. People who detest God and His ways go there. Readers learn from the Pergamum church of the popularity of the devil's ways, but these must not be tolerated. The devil's ways must be revealed for what they are—the wiles of a defeated enemy leading on the broad path to the destruction of body and soul. Everyone must choose carefully whom they serve. If it is God, the devil must be fought; God will provide all that is needed to resist and endure the battle.

> No temptation has overtaken you that is not common to men. God is faithful, and he will not let you be tempted beyond your ability, but with the temptation he will also provide the way of escape, that you may be able to endure it. (1 Cor. 10:13)

Ruins inside Akhisar, Turkey, possible site of the church in Thyatira.

But I, brothers, could not address you as spiritual people, but as people of the flesh, as infants in Christ. I fed you with milk, not solid food, for you were not ready for it. And even now you are not yet ready, for you are still of the flesh. For while there is jealousy and strife among you, are you not of the flesh and behaving only in a human way? (1 Cor. 3:1–3)

CHAPTER 6

Thyatira—Accepting Sin—of the Flesh

And to the angel of the church in Thyatira write: "The words of the Son of God, who has eyes like a flame of fire, and whose feet are like burnished bronze. "I know your works, your love and faith and service and patient endurance, and that your latter works exceed the first. But I have this against you, that you tolerate that woman Jezebel, who calls herself a prophetess and is teaching and seducing my servants to practice sexual immorality and to eat food sacrificed to idols. I gave her time to repent, but she refuses to repent of her sexual immorality. Behold, I will throw her onto a sickbed, and those who commit adultery with her I will throw into great tribulation, unless they repent of her works, and I will strike her children dead. And all the churches will know that I am he who searches mind and heart, and I will give to each of you according to your works. But to the rest of you in Thyatira, who do not hold this teaching, who have not learned what some call the deep things of Satan, to you I say, I do not lay on you any other burden. Only hold fast what you have until I come. The one who conquers and who keeps my works until the end, to him I will give authority over the nations, and he will rule them with a rod of iron, as when earthen pots are broken in pieces, even as I myself have received authority from my Father. And I will give him the morning star. He who has an ear, let him hear what the Spirit says to the churches." (Rev. 2:18–29)

While we occupy these bodies of flesh, we experience all that the world, the devil, or God can bring, from the most debased evil to absolute and perfect love. Ultimately, through their physical bodies, many learn that they are more than physical beings—they are also spiritual and eternal beings. The seven letters help readers understand how humans are capable of both great malevolence and great benevolence. Thyatira's letter, the central letter, illustrates how most sin results from fleshly needs and desires. It helps us understand how easy it is to accept sin which affects body, soul, and eternal life.

Where in the World Is Thyatira?

Thyatira or Thyateira, close to the Lycus River, is fifty-two miles southeast of Pergamum and forty miles north of Sardis. It is approximately two hundred thirty miles south of Istanbul. Located on an ancient Asia Minor trade route that bordered Lydia and Mysia, it was the outer military defense to Pergamum as part of the Roman Empire. Today the county town of Akhisar (meaning *white castle*) surrounds and covers most of its ancient ruins.

Thyatira did not reach the status of other cities, but it was an important economic industrial and agricultural center of the northern Aegean region. It was well known for textile production: wool and linen, wool and fabric painting, leather manufacturing, shoe making, bronze and silver working, pottery, and dyes (especially a costly purple variety). Thyatira was immensely popular because of its trade guilds that supported workers in their respective livelihoods.

History and Archaeology

The smallest archaeological site of the Revelation churches, Thyatira's ruins shed light on the letter that it received. Turkey has many active archaeological sites, but most of Thyatira's ruins remain buried beneath Akhisar's buildings and streets maybe due to massive earthquakes in 25/24 BC, 17 AD, and 178/179 AD. The fenced-in city block is surrounded by a metropolis of approximately one hundred twenty thousand residents, according to Turkish estimates.

According to Epiphanius (Refutation of All Heresies 51.33), around 200 AD Thyatira was Christian but aligned with the Montanist movement (a schismatic second- to ninth-century prophetic sect). The city was lost to the world after Emperor Caracalla's visit in 214 AD until October 8, 1670, when the British consul in Smyrna, Paul Rycaut, rode into it after visiting Pergamum. Rycaut saw pillars, rare sculptures, inscriptions, broken stones, and the Greek word *Thyateira*.

Two marble bases that honored a well-known citizen showed the prominence of trade guilds. The last line inscribed on the bases indicated sponsorship by the fullers[64] for one pillar and by the wool workers for the other.[65]

Thyatira's cemetery and hospital mound remains reveal sculptures, mosaics, frescos, and glass and ceramic artifacts from the Roman and Byzantine periods. Excavations also reveal an "early occupation dating back to 3,000 BC."[66] A main building has been dated to the Roman period between the second and sixth centuries AD.

---

[64] David Elton Graves, "What is the Madder with Lydia's Purple? A Reexamination of the Purpurarii in Thyatira and Philippi," January 2017, ResearchGate. The fullers cleaned and finished the cloth before dyeing it. This was an expensive process which only the wealthy could afford.

[65] Wilson, *Biblical Turkey*, 323.

[66] Mark R. Fairchild, *Christian Origins in Ephesus and Asia Minor* (Istanbul, Turkey: Arkeoege, 2015), 171.

An inscribed marble antiquity at the excavation site in Thyatira.

The oldest written detail about ancient Thyatira comes from the third century BC and reports that the name *Thyateira* originated with the Lydian *teira*, meaning fortress or town. This suggests that Thyateira had been an important settlement since the Lydian period. Others say that Thyatira was settled mainly by Macedonians who worshipped and made offerings to Seleukos/Nicotor. Its name can also refer to the castle of Thya because, before the time of Nicator, Thyatira was regarded as a holy city. A temple of the ancient Lydian sun god, Tyrimnus, identified with the Greek god Apollo, was located there and games were held near the temple in his honor.

The Lydians were the first to mint coins. Early Thyatiran coins depicting Apollo and Tyrimnus holding a double-headed battle ax have been found. Other gods and goddesses, including Artemis and Asclepius, were worshipped in Thyatira, but Apollo was the most important, as he was the patron god of trade guilds. Another temple in Thyatira dedicated to the worship of the Chaldean goddess Sambethe was said to have been frequented by a popular prophetess who claimed to receive knowledge directly from Sambethe. Some believe that this is the Jezebel for which Jesus rebukes Thyatira.

Evidence of Paul or John visiting Thyatira is circumstantial. Luke records a Lydia from Thyatira who was converted and baptized by Paul in Philippi, the first place in Macedonia (Europe) where Paul preached (Acts 16:14–15). Little is known about Lydia, but she or family members may have started the church in Philippi. We do not know definitively how Thyatira became a Christian town, but we do know that a woman named Lydia, a seller of purple, from the town of Thyatira, was converted to Christianity in Philippi.

Thyatira was renowned for its trade guilds, which were the center of community life. More guilds were present there than in other comparable cities in Asia Minor. The trade guilds were more than unions or social clubs. They linked daily work life with the temple worship of pagan gods and goddesses, especially Apollo. These guilds held banquets in the temples. After ritual meals, revelers regularly engaged in sexually immoral acts on the couches.[67] The

---

[67] Wilson, *Biblical Turkey*, 322.

guilds were so influential that non-members were unable to secure jobs. It would have been exceedingly difficult to be faithful to Jesus and be a guild member.

Inwardly Digesting Revelation 2:18–29

Revelation 2:18

> And to the angel of the church in Thyatira write: The words of the Son of God, who has eyes like a flame of fire, and whose feet are like burnished bronze.

Jesus's opening words to the church in Thyatira grabbed their attention because the "words of the Son of God" would remind them of Thyatiran temple worship of the sun god Apollo, son of Zeus, the chief Greek god and father of all gods. These words would have been even more relevant to Christians because Jesus refers to Himself as having "eyes like a flame of fire" and "feet like burnished bronze"; these details echo the vision of the Son of Man in Revelation 1:14–15. This description should not impact our visualization of Jesus's physical being; we know nothing about what Jesus looked like. John's language in Revelation is metaphorical. Later in Revelation 19:12, the phrase "eyes like a flame of fire" describes the rider on the white horse, who is Jesus.

Much of the industry in Thyatira would have used fire to heat water for dyeing cloth, for leather working, for making pottery, and for melting and shaping metals. As the Thyatirans worked in various industries that used fire, they would have been familiar with what flames of fire did to metals and other materials. They would have known the importance of being careful with fire. "Eyes like a flame of fire" indicates Jesus's omniscience, His all-seeing power. This phrase reminded the church that Jesus could see into their lives and works and that nothing could be hidden from Him, not even behind trade guild or temple doors. Jesus's fire is an all-consuming fire, capable of destroying anything—even man. Apollo was no match for the Lord Jesus Christ.

At the time of the writing of Revelation, bronze, one of the toughest metals, was more economical than gold or silver. Because bronze was less malleable and less corrosive than copper, working with bronze in Thyatira was profitable. It was used in Roman armor, such as shields and helmets; weapons, such as swords and spears; and to mint coins and make ornamental statues and jewelry.

In the Bible, gold represents God, whereas bronze represents sinful humanity and God's righteous judgment through Christ. "Feet like burnished bronze" signifies Jesus's strength as the only sinless human and His power in judging people and trampling out their sin.[68] Ezekiel refers to God's glory as being like burnished bronze (Ezek. 1:7). Daniel describes the terrifying man of his vision as having "arms and legs like the gleam of burnished bronze" (Dan. 10:6). This heavenly messenger was like the Son of Man, but he was not Jesus. Christians knew that God would trample sin under His feet and eventually punish unrepentant sinners.

Whether the bronze is polished or burnished is unimportant; what is important is its shine. Because bronze reflects light, it was used to make mirrors which were quite significant to the Israelites. Mirrors may stimulate Christians to reflect on their spiritual nature as well as on their appearance. Additionally, bronze may signify the passage of time. Metaphorically, mirrors reflect the Israelites' physical and spiritual journeys from the time of creation. They also may symbolize Christians' faith through the light of Jesus.

Israelite mirrors were used in God's sanctuary, the Temple. Exodus records how Bezalel, one of the craftsman God skilled with the ability to build His Holy Temple through the Holy Spirit, "made the basin of bronze and its stand of bronze, from the mirrors of the ministering women who ministered in the entrance of the tent of meeting" (Exod. 38:8). These women would have had good-quality,

---

[68] "The Meaning of Bronze in the Bible," accessed October 8, 2019, https://www.oneforisrael.org/bible-based-teaching-from-israel/the-meaning-of-bronze-in-the-bible/.

highly polished pieces of bronze, taken out of Egypt during the exodus as they left for the promised land (Exod. 12:36).

Some writers have extrapolated references of Jesus to *burnished bronze* as meaning that Jesus was a person of color, as bronze ages naturally to a golden brown. The Bible does not reveal anything definitive about Jesus's appearance. Jesus is Savior to all who call upon Him, regardless of nationality. The most important point we must take from any metaphorical reference to Jesus's physical appearance is that He appeared on this earth in full humanity. Jesus had a fully human birth, lived a fully human life, and suffered a fully human death. "Feet like burnished bronze" appropriately refers to Jesus's full humanity because bronze portrays humanity as well as judgment. Jesus's burnished feet reflect the difference that His life has made to the whole of humanity, as He shines light on and tramples out sin through His sacrificial atonement for Christians' sins, because He is also fully divine.

Revelation 2:19

> *I know your works, your love and faith and service and patient endurance, and that your latter works exceed the first.*

Jesus commended the Thyatiran church for its works, love, faith, service, patient endurance, and progress. He looked favorably on them because they worked hard and did many things right. Unlike the Ephesian church, they loved God first and endured pressure and persecution for their beliefs.

Those refusing to join guilds and participate in their pagan and sexual revelry suffered consequences, as do faithful Christians today. Some probably could not secure employment. Christian families were poor, hungry, homeless, and shunned. They would not eat food that had been sacrificed to idols, certainly not in the temples as an act of worship. They could not—to do so would go against their faith. However, if eating this food sustained their faithful bodies, and if they found it without compromising their faith or being a stumbling block to others, God may not have condemned them.

Being commended for its works spoke highly of this church. Its Christians gave of themselves for others out of love for them, which is the love that Jesus teaches all Christians to have. They learned to love strangers, the downtrodden, and even their enemies. This church served people as though they were serving God. Their faith was alive and growing; their good works were bigger and greater than they had been in the beginning. They were being sanctified daily in their faith.

Thyatira's good qualities were like those of the church in Thessalonica, which Paul praised as "remembering before our God and Father your work of faith and labor of love and steadfastness of hope in our Lord Jesus Christ" (1 Thess. 1:3). Revelation 2:19 must have provided hope to church members, but not for all of them, and not for the whole church, because the remainder of the letter contains chastisement and warning.

Revelation 2:20–22

> But I have this against you, that you tolerate that woman Jezebel, who calls herself a prophetess and is teaching and seducing my servants to practice sexual immorality and to eat food sacrificed to idols. I gave her time to repent, but she refuses to repent of her sexual immorality. Behold, I will throw her onto a sickbed, and those who commit adultery with her I will throw into great tribulation, unless they repent of her works …

Some in the Thyatira church worked diligently for God; others sinned against Him. Jesus knew that the idolatrous prophetess Jezebel had seduced some church members into being sexually immoral, eating food sacrificed to idols, and worshipping other gods.

Jezebel appealed to their fleshly desires: to eat whatever they wanted and to lust after and have sexual relations with whomever and whenever they wanted. Eating food that had been sacrificed to idols was a problem in Pergamum, but it was a greater problem in Thyatira, where a priestess enticed Christians to sin in many ways. Jesus warned that permitting Jezebel to teach errors was wrong. Her false teaching drew people away from God into idolatry and sin. The evil in Thyatira was not outside this church—it resided within it. Some within the church sinned with Jezebel. Some who did not sin with her, however, sinned by not correcting her and those sinning with her.

Ahab, the seventh king of the northern kingdom of Israel, had a wife, Jezebel, whose father, Ethbaal, was king of the Sidonians. The wicked Jezebel convinced Ahab to worship the nature god Baal. She seduced people into following her pagan god's ways by eating food sacrificed to idols. The four hundred fifty prophets of Baal challenged by Elijah and the four hundred prophets of Asherah ate at Jezebel's table (1 Kgs. 18:19).

The Jezebel of Thyatira may refer to someone like King Ahab's wife or the Jezebel dedicated to worshipping the Chaldean goddess Sambethe or someone else. The name "Jezebel" is usually equated with sin and evil, especially sexual promiscuity, and people like this Jezebel are sometimes referred to as having a Jezebel spirit. Whoever she was, Jezebel needed to be dealt with rightly by the church. Fighting sin and heresy that is instigated by the devil is often more difficult than battling the devil himself. People's sins can be more insidious, because the people themselves, like the alluring Jezebels of the Bible and of the world, are attractive, beguiling, and captivating.

Although the church grew more each day in faith, some members fell deeper into a pit of depravity with Jezebel. Their good works could not save them. Those who knew Jesus were washed in His blood and obedient to His teachings. The good works of those associating with Jezebel, her sexual immorality, and her eating of food sacrificed to idols were useless, because her sin had become part of their lives.

Much worse than tolerating Jezebel was sinning as she sinned. Jezebel would suffer the torments of hell eternally because she did not turn from her wicked ways. Likewise, those following her will be found guilty too when Jesus says that He does not know them. Some will be found guilty of fornication, of eating meat sacrificed to idols, and/or of allowing Jezebel's false teaching to continue. Jesus warns that accepting sexual sin grieves God. The Thyatira church did many things right, but by being silent when it should have spoken out against Jezebel and her sin, it was condemned.

Because of the numerous pagan gods being worshipped in Thyatira, an abundance of meat had to be thrown away if it was uneaten. The Romans' public feasts, which made meat available to the general population, was an efficient way to dispose of these sacrificed animals while helping to feed the poor. This was good for pagans but not for hungry Christians.

Revelation 2:23

> ... and I will strike her children dead. And all the churches will know that I am he who searches mind and heart, and I will give to each of you according to your works.

The Lord gave Jezebel time to repent and the church time to rebuke her and return to orthodoxy. Because she did not repent, and the church did not discipline her, both continued in their sin. All were under Jesus's judgment. Jezebel and the church were in jeopardy of losing their children because of wickedness and hardheartedness, just as Pharaoh had lost his oldest son. The loss of eternal life is worse than physical death. All seven churches and others in the vicinity of each would soon know that Jesus is the One who searches minds and hearts and gives to each according to their deeds.

Revelation 2:24–25

> But to the rest of you in Thyatira, who do not hold this teaching, who have not learned what some call the deep things of Satan, to you I say, I do not lay on

*you any other burden. Only hold fast what you have
until I come.*

Jesus expected the Christians in Thyatira, those who did not hold to Jezebel's wicked ways and who had not been corrupted by her evil, to stand firm in their faith. He knew who they were, and He encouraged them to stay strong in the gospel. Those happy in the Lord knew that they had nothing to fear. Standing strong in the Lord may have been easy for them, but it must have been difficult to watch others wallow in sin. The fervent prayers of the faithful may have helped some.

Revelation 2:26–29

> *The one who conquers and who keeps my works until
> the end, to him I will give authority over the nations,
> and he will rule them with a rod of iron, as when
> earthen pots are broken in pieces, even as I myself
> have received authority from my Father. And I will
> give him the morning star. He who has an ear, let him
> hear what the Spirit says to the churches.*

Jesus refers to those who stay strong in their faith as conquerors or overcomers. Satan will not defeat them. The faithful are part of Christ's victorious body. With and in Jesus, they will rule the nations, as God has given them authority to do so. Conquerors would be given the morning star, Jesus Himself (Rev. 22:16). Those victorious in Christ will live with Him forever. "Ruling with a rod of iron" would have been significant to this church, especially for the pottery makers. Defective pottery, those cracked or flawed pieces, were smashed with rods of iron so that they could be reworked into new pots. Jesus, the ultimate potter, was working on their hearts.

Putting the Pieces Together

In ancient times, basic needs were met by hunting, fishing, raising animals, growing and gathering what was required, and cutting trees for firewood and building materials. Over time, people became specialized in the use of local resources. Systems of barter and trade grew, generally ensuring that all were cared for, for the good of the community. Parts of fields were purposefully left to be gleaned by the poor. Mining and working with metal and minerals became regular trades. In the first century, men worked as farmers, shepherds, wool makers and weavers, potters, fishermen, carpenters, metal workers, and soldiers to provide for their families. In Thyatira, this list would have included those procuring dye and dyeing cloth and those employed in the temples and trade guilds where workers worshipped and socialized with colleagues. Sexual immorality was common, especially in temples where temple prostitutes were part of the worship.

The issue of eating food sacrificed to idols arose in Paul's day about fifty years before the writing of Revelation (Acts 15:29; 1 Cor. 8:1–13), but it had been a Jewish problem before that (Exod. 32:6; 34:15; Num. 25:2; Ezek. 23:37, 39). Paul did not always deem it inappropriate, as sometimes it was acceptable to eat food that had been sacrificed to idols. Sometimes it was not. It would have been inappropriate for Christians to eat this food in temples during pagan worship events or drunken orgies. Expectations did not change between the writing of the letters to the Corinthians and the letters to the seven churches. The main difference with Thyatira is that Jezebel, a pagan prophetess and a fornicator, was in the church, and eating food sacrificed to idols was idolatry.

Eating such food may not have been a problem for Christians if Jesus were Lord of their lives. For Thyatiran Christians, who were without income because they refused to participate in the trade guilds' idolatry, eating anything would have strengthened them to live to proclaim the good news of the gospel. Eating food sacrificed to idols would not have compromised their faith but was a way to feed their families. God may have provided food for them in this way, but not in a public place or at a pagan temple or immoral festival where it would have been a stumbling block to non-Christians.

Temptations of the flesh are personal battles between gratifying fleshly desires and obeying God. Many give in to temptations, especially if the devil is involved, because he is a master at luring and enticing people. Most sins of the flesh provide immediate gratification and, therefore, are addictive. Addiction makes it easy to offend repeatedly and accept fleshly sin as innate desires requiring fulfillment rather than being anti-God and needing to be fought with His help. The Bible condemns all sin and says that God requires obedience. If we love God, we will study Scripture and be obedient.

In 1 Samuel 13, King Saul disobeyed God's commands that were given to him through the prophet Samuel regarding the Philistines. Once again, in 1 Samuel 15:22–23, Saul felt that he knew better than God and did not destroy the Amalekites as Samuel had instructed him: "Has the Lord as great delight in burnt offerings and sacrifices, as in obeying the voice of the Lord? Behold, to obey is better than sacrifice, and to listen than the fat of rams." Saul thought that he could please God by doing things his way, by offering worship and sacrifice outside of God's will. Saul sinned against God when he did not kill the Amalekites as God had commanded. Saul's sin was like divination. His presumption of knowing better than God was the sin of idolatry. Because Saul had rejected God's direction through Samuel, God rejected him as king.

Afterwards some of the best spoils of war were sacrificed to God in Gilgal. God's purpose for the Amalekites' destruction was to root out paganism, which is an abomination to Him. God required Saul's obedience. He did not want Saul to solve the problem but to listen to Samuel, His messenger. Saul, ruled by sinful fleshly desires, wanted his own way, not God's, and his sin defeated him.

Some who profess to be Christians are like Saul. They want things in their time and in their way and teach that going against God is permissible for Christians because all their sins were dealt with at the cross. Going against God, they think, will not hurt them. In addition to being a dubious biblical interpretation, one must question how anyone could profess to know and love God yet persist in going against everything that He is. God's love and grace are not of the world. Many relationships have been destroyed by such cheap love and cheap grace. Only God can tell us, show us, and give us His love, the costliest love in the world, and His grace.

Jesus supplies all that we need to defeat the sins of the flesh. His human life fulfilled the Father's will, not His own. Although Jesus is God, when He walked the earth, He chose, in full humanity, to obey His Father. As a man, Jesus was tempted as we are, but He did not sin. In His flesh, Jesus never tolerated or accepted sin. He had mercy on sinners, but He did not hide God's truth about sin. Jesus did not want the torture and humiliation of the cross, but, in His flesh, He obeyed God so that all who believe in Him will have eternal life. Believing in Jesus means loving Father, Son, and Holy Spirit because of who they are and what they love. It is a call to obey as Jesus did.

Accepting Sin: Of the Flesh

> But I say, walk by the Spirit, and you will not gratify the desires of the flesh. For the desires of the flesh are against the Spirit, and the desires of the Spirit are against the flesh, for these are opposed to each other, to keep you from doing the things you want to do. (Gal. 5:16–17)

Paul also wrote letters to seven churches: Rome, Corinth, Galatia, Ephesus, Philippi, Colossae, and Thessalonica. His letter to Galatia, written around 48 AD, admonished Christians to fight the sins of the flesh by being led by the Holy Spirit so that they would not be under the law. In verse 19, he listed the works of the flesh: "sexual immorality, impurity, sensuality, idolatry, sorcery, enmity, strife, jealousy, fits of anger, rivalries, dissensions, divisions, envy, drunkenness, orgies, and things like these." Christians were warned that, if they engaged in such activities, they would not inherit the kingdom of God. Thyatira's letter is the longest and most important, as it addresses the flesh.

A vast chasm exists between needs and wants. What some regard as needs are not. What some desire and lust after are deadly, and not of God. God created and made the world and everything in it, but for a time He allows the devil to rule. The devil entices humans to crave what is against God's created good order and encourages sinful physical desires. People increasingly fall victim to what they want, as the devil becomes increasingly desperate to lure them further from Christ and God's values.

The devil ruled in Jesus's day but was unsuccessful in enticing Jesus to fall into sin. In His humanity, Jesus knew God's laws perfectly and taught God's will. Most who answer God's call to ministry work hard to fight temptation, but some fail miserably, often leaving behind a flock of Christians working for God against a backlash of sin.

The greatest sins involve idolatry. Idolatry breaks at least the first and second commandments. Jesus describes how sexual immorality and murder are heinous sins of the flesh. Everyone must care for their physical needs and those of their families but God must always be first. As in first-century Thyatira, today's Christians, tempted to compromise their faith to ensure their livelihood, know that they must not.[69]

Idolatry

Pleasure is often linked to idolatry, as it was with Jezebel, and is doubly sinful. To worship anyone or anything other than God is an abomination to Him. Anyone who leads a person away from God into

---

[69] Some Christians forced to move away from their communities for employment share stories of why they quit well-paying jobs to escape sinful lifestyles. Anyone moving to a new community is expected to fit in. Travelling with a band or music group or relocating for employment is a difficult lifestyle which some find that they must leave when it means taking up anything counter to God: alcohol, drugs, gambling, and/or sexual immorality. God is with them in their struggle to remain faithful to Him and their families.

sin, as Balaam did with the Pergamum church, and we may infer the Nicolaitans also did, is betting on your accepting them and their sins:

> The description of the teachings of the woman prophet "Jezebel" was identical to the teachings of Balaam, who was misleading the church at Pergamum. Both were enticing Christians to engage in acts of immorality, to eat things sacrificed to idols, and to be involved in sorcery and divination (Revelation 2:14 & 20). If this Balaam were connected to the Nicolaitans (as Revelation 2:15 may imply) then we should assume that this Jezebel was also a leader within the Nicolaitan movement.[70]

The Nicolaitans, Balaam's sorcery commissioned by Balak, and Jezebel point to one source—evil, against God, of the devil, and equivalent to idolatry.

Some Christians believe that they have immunity to sin and are entitled to all sorts of "blessings" because they are "saved." Some "Christian" leaders believe that their entitlement spills over into an opulent lifestyle, leading to greed—which is not of God. Material well-being itself is not sinful, but when wealth is idolized, it separates persons from God. Christians must be good stewards of all resources that God has entrusted to them, but they are not assured of a pain-free, wealthy life.

Many would rather blame God and be angry with Him than admit their own wrongdoing, even when everything turns out well. This struggle of human will against God's will is idolatry. Admitting sin is difficult. Life, however, is filled with choices and concomitant risks. Those who fornicate with Jezebel and her illegitimate children, which may represent those in Thyatira who exhibited her idolatrous and occultic behaviors, her spiritual offspring, will share in her suffering unless they repent. Sinners will reap the consequences of their sins but will not lose their souls if they repent and change.

---

[70] Fairchild, *Christian Origins in Ephesus and Asia Minor,* 170.

Sexual Immorality

For many years sexual sin was what came to mind first when anyone spoke of sins of the flesh because it was regarded as worse than stealing food, overeating, being materialistic, and having surplus. Today in many circles sexual sin does not exist. Those who believe it does may vilify it according to degree, but the Bible does not differentiate between adultery, homosexual acts, or fornication, all of which are sexual relations outside the biblical definition of marriage between a man and a woman. The Bible teaches that all sin causes pain and heartache to its participants. Its commandments and laws describe abortion, adultery, fornication, homosexuality, and prostitution as sins of the flesh. Christians are better equipped to stand against sin if they are not battling another sin (i.e., arrogance, doubt, self-righteousness, or pride).

Sex always gets attention because of the pleasure associated with the release of the hormones oxytocin and dopamine. Like other physical pleasures, it is addictive, because our bodies crave pleasure. Until the twentieth century, children were conceived solely through the coupling of a male and a female. Sexual intercourse, therefore, was associated with pregnancy and creation. God's plan is for a man and a woman to leave their families and create their own family. Sex matters greatly to God: He created it.

Having a Jezebel spirit is one way of referring to someone powerful who is wallowing in sin, especially sexual sin. This term describes any seductive, promiscuous person, regardless of gender. David, the greatest Israelite king, sinned, but he repented and lived (Ps. 91). His son Solomon in contrast, may be lost forever, as the Bible does not record his repenting of his relations with foreign women and idolizing their gods (I Kgs. 11). Some believe that Solomon wrote Ecclesiastes, which admonishes those who live a wayward life, but God alone knows the author. The Jezebels of our day seem to be more insidious than those of either Ahab's day or in the first century.

Sex has only ever been limited by the imagination. What once happened in private, however, has become far more blatant.

Increasingly looser sexual morals shock fewer and fewer people. Sexual sins are more visible and ever available via technology. Little is kept from children, who are easy pornographic prey. The God-ordained family is replaced by any combination of lifestyle. Undesired conception is terminated without a second thought, while rampant sexually transmitted diseases are treated. The devil's latest ploy to destroy biological gender, the basis of God's creation, surprises even some of the most progressive liberals. These issues support God and His Word rather than the devil and his lies.[71] Much of the "church" accepts "cultural repositioning" as the world does. It no longer teaches the biblical definitions of marriage, family, or sexuality.

What do Christians do when church leaders themselves are deviant, biblically deficient, worldly, and as self-seeking as the public? It is understandable why many who attend church are confused and discouraged. Few today believe that God made us with qualities like Him and gifted us to be actively part of His creation. But neither God nor His Word changes. Biblical advice is always sound advice to Christians. "Christians" who not only tolerate sexual sin but accept and often promote it are not part of God's family.[72] They belong to the flesh and are of the world, under the leadership of the devil:

> For this is the will of God, your sanctification: that you abstain from sexual immorality; that each one of you know how to control his own body in holiness and honor, not in the passion of lust like the Gentiles who do not know God; that no one transgress and wrong his brother in this matter, because the Lord is an avenger in all these things, as we told you beforehand and solemnly warned you. For God has not called us for impurity, but in holiness. Therefore, whoever

---

[71] Hormone therapy and surgery do not change a person's DNA. Education regarding gender and sexuality, including, but not limited to, gender assignment at birth, intersexuality, sexual disorders, and transgenderism must be studied and honestly talked about in churches, and in the light of the Bible.

[72] In recent years, the term *toleration* has broadened beyond acceptance to promotion.

disregards this, disregards not man but God, who gives his Holy Spirit to you. (1 Thess. 4:3–8)

A Bed of Suffering—Murder of Body and Soul

"Behold, I will throw her onto a sickbed, and those who commit adultery with her I will throw into great tribulation, unless they repent of her works" (Rev. 2:22). The Jezebel of verse 21 was given the opportunity to repent but did not. She and those sinning with her will suffer acutely if they do not repent of their sinful ways. Everything that everyone does has consequences, but sin is against God and punishable by eternal death if we do not repent. Trials of the flesh include sickness, hardship, suffering, and death, but those washed in Christ's atoning blood have the hope of eternal life after their deaths.

In the twenty-first century, there is no place to be physically safe from guns, knives, or violence. Murder breaks the sixth commandment, but worse than murder of the body is murder of the soul. Jezebel and all who lead others into sin kill souls, because the souls of all unrepentant sinners die. Jesus said to fear those who destroy body and soul in hell. Christians must teach God's truth in love to fight the world's Jezebels:

> So have no fear of them, for nothing is covered that will not be revealed, or hidden that will not be known. What I tell you in the dark, say in the light, and what you hear whispered, proclaim on the housetops. And do not fear those who kill the body but cannot kill the soul. Rather fear him who can destroy both soul and body in hell. (Matt. 10:26–28)

The devil, the world, and the flesh tempt, but people choose to sin. The idiom, "If you make your bed hard you must lie on it," applies here. Poor choices often lead to pain and suffering. Only God can remove everyone's bed of suffering but He often does not. There is no peace apart from God and nowhere to flee from His sight. Thyatira's letter reinforces that, as it pertains to livelihood (trade guilds, unions, work ethic), leisure time, pleasure, and sin. Much in Jesus's message to Thyatira causes us to rethink how we might be living for God or far from Him. If we accept what God deems detestable and evil and do not repent, we will not be in heaven with Him after we die. We cannot be, as God and sin do not coexist. Heaven is God's home. Everything there is of Him. If we accept what God detests, we will also detest heaven.

Thyatira in Our Time

Our flesh, what we know best of all, is not evil. It is a gift from God that enables us to live to know Him and His Son, Jesus, whose life, teachings, sacrificial death, and resurrection saves us from sin and transforms us into God's children. The Thyatiran letter shows that sins of the flesh cannot be accepted if we love God. If we build a god in our image, with our selfish ways, we do not reflect who God is or what He desires, as everything revolves around us. Battling the flesh is difficult because sin is continuously promoted by the world and it knocks on the doors of our hearts. The only way to be safe from soul-murderers is to walk in the Holy Spirit through a strong relationship with Jesus. God will not change to be like us. He loves us and listens to us, He sends the Holy Spirit and angels to help us, but God will never accommodate our sin.

The letter to Thyatira is relevant because we love what we know, and we know nothing better than our own bodies. The indwelling Holy Spirit prompts Christians to live beyond self-centeredness, sexual immorality, and pride and beyond even what the world considers reasonable. Christians, both rich and poor, live wholly for God.

> "All flesh is like grass and all its glory like the flower of grass. The grass withers, and the flower falls, but the word of the Lord remains forever." (1 Pet. 1:24–25)[73]

---

[73] See James 1:9–11. Both James and Peter first heard of or read this scriptural wisdom in Isaiah 40:6–8.

The ruins of the Temple to Artemis, Sardis, with the acropolis behind it.

Do not love the world or the things of the world. If anyone loves the world, the love of the Father is not in him. For all that is in the world—the desires of the flesh and the desires of the eyes and pride in possessions—is not from the Father but it is from the world. (1 John 2:15–16)

CHAPTER 7

Sardis—Promoting Sin—of the World

And to the angel of the church in Sardis write: "The words of him who has the seven spirits of God and the seven stars.

"I know your works. You have the reputation of being alive, but you are dead. Wake up, and strengthen what remains and is about to die, for I have not found your works complete in the sight of my God. Remember, then, what you received and heard. Keep it, and repent. If you will not wake up, I will come like a thief, and you will not know at what hour I will come against you. Yet you have still a few names in Sardis, people who have not soiled their garments, and they will walk with me in white, for they are worthy. The one who conquers will be clothed thus in white garments, and I will never blot his name out of the book of life. I will confess his name before my Father and before his angels. He who has an ear, let him hear what the Spirit says to the churches." (Rev. 3:1–6)

Acceptance of sin leads to its promotion. The people of Sardis, home of the fifth church, were affluent, influenced by power and prestige, and enjoyed enlightened exchange and debate, culture, sports, and entertainment. They gained the world by compromising their values and beliefs and lived together peacefully. Its church was not awake. Lulled into complacency, it could not hear Jesus's voice but was on its way to losing its soul.

Where in the World Is Sardis?

Sardis was like two cities living as one: one on a plateau, the other on a plain. Also called Sardes or Sart, Sardis is home to about five thousand today. Located at the foot of Mount Tmolus in Western Anatolia, present-day Manisa province, Sardis is about forty miles southeast of Thyatira and twenty-seven miles northwest of Philadelphia (Ataşehir) at the end of what was the Royal Road. The city was watered by the Pactolus River, which was known for its golden sand due to the gold dust coming down from Mount Tmolus.

History and Archaeology

Ancient Sardis was the powerful capital of the kingdom of Lydia. Its last king, Croesus, who ruled from about 560 to 547 BC, was the first person to strike and issue pure gold and silver coins for use in the marketplace. The metallurgists of Croesus's day had found a new way to separate gold and silver such that each retained its purity. Croesus's father, King Alyattes, had minted the world's first coins.

Sardis was home to one of the Seven Wonders of the Ancient World, the huge temple to the Greek goddess Artemis, twice the size of the Greek Parthenon, paid for by Croesus. The goddess Cybele and the god Zeus were also worshipped in Sardis. The city grew to be an important commercial and trade center where Greek Ionian settlers and Mesopotamians met as intellectuals, sharing their ideas and beliefs.

Thought to be impregnable due to its citadel atop the acropolis, Sardis became important to the Persians after its hilltop was conquered by Cyrus the Great in 546 BC. The acropolis was conquered similarly by the Seleucids under Antiochus III in 218 BC. Destroyed by an earthquake in 17 AD, Sardis was quickly rebuilt.

It remained one of the greatest cities in Asia Minor until the later Byzantine period. The people of Sardis were known for how well they got along with, and supported, one another.

The archaeological site close to the Pactolus River contains the ruins of a temple to Artemis which housed a fourth-century Byzantine church. Little remains of the ancient Lydian fortifications atop the acropolis, but ruins of Sardes Castle, a seventh century Byzantine structure, can still be explored there.[74]

Excavations at a second archaeological site reveal many late Roman houses and shops, the most impressive Jewish synagogue in the western diaspora complete with mosaic floors, a major Roman bath-gymnasium complex, and a library. Artifacts found in and around the Byzantine shops situated along what was called Marble Avenue led scholars to believe that they had Jewish, Christian, and secular owners.

The Jewish synagogue is in the midst of what was a social center which included a shopping area adjoining a library and Roman bath-gymnasium complex. Exercise and sports, especially competitive games, were popular, and keeping in top physical shape especially so. This sports complex was not only the center for exercise and sport but it was also a place of camaraderie, mixing sport, play, and a pagan lifestyle. Winners wore white and were presented with a crown of olive branches. The synagogue's eclectic mixture of religious items indicated that synagogue life had integrated into Roman civic and pagan life. The supports of a marble table from which the Hebrew Scripture was read were decked with Roman eagles that held thunderbolts. At each end of the table stood two pairs of seventh- to sixth-century BC lions, perhaps from the temple of Cybele.[75]

According to tradition, Sardis was the first city in the area to be converted by John. The most-noted Christian of the city is Bishop Melito, a Hellenistic Jew and early church father who died in 180

[74] "Sardes Castle," accessed October 21, 2020, www.castles.nl/sardes-castle.
[75] "Cybele Altar, Sardis," accessed December 4, 2020, www.sacred-destinations.com/turkey/sardis-altar-of-cybele.

AD and was buried at Sardis. Melito's literary works, most of which have been lost, held great prominence, according to Clement of Alexandria, Origen, and Eusebius. Melito's Old Testament canon was the earliest known, similar to the Jewish Tanakh and the Protestant canon, according to Jerome. Influenced by John's teachings, Melito too believed in the unity of Jesus and His Father.[76]

Remains of the synagogue floor with the gymnasium in the background, Sardis.

[76] "Melito of Sardis," accessed July 1, 2020, https://www.cogwriter.com/melito.htm, and "Melito of Sardis," accessed July 1, 2020, https://en.wikipedia.org/wiki/Melito_of_Sardis. Melito's most-famous writings centered around the celebration of Easter. He believed that Easter coincided with the Jewish Passover on the fourteenth of Nisan and that the Christian Passover should be celebrated on that date. This practice was overturned by the Council of Nicaea in 325 AD.

Revelation 3:1

> And to the angel of the church in Sardis write: *The words of him who has the seven spirits of God and the seven stars. I know your works. You have the reputation of being alive, but you are dead.*

Jesus did not have a single commendation for the Sardis church. The letter opens with a description of Jesus having the seven spirits of God and the seven stars, or angels, signifying His spiritual perfection. Jesus refers to Himself as having the seven spirits of God, or seven gifts of the Holy Spirit, found in Isaiah 11:1–3 and in the Hebrew Masoretic text[77] in which the righteous branch of Jesse (King David's father) rests upon and bears fruit. The seven spirits of God are wisdom, understanding, counsel, might, knowledge, fear of the Lord, and piety (or reverence, added by the church fathers). Instead of a commendation, Jesus told the church in Sardis that it was dead. They might have thought that they were alive, and they may have had the reputation of being a strong church because everyone around them may have thought that they were alive, but they were not. *They were dead.* Can anything be worse for a church than to be told that it is dead?

Revelation 3:2

> *Wake up, and strengthen what remains and is about to die, for I have not found your works complete in the sight of my God.*

---

[77] The Masoretic text is "the authoritative Hebrew Aramaic text of the 24 books of the Tanakh in Rabbinic Judaism ... primarily copied, edited and distributed by a group of Jews known as the Masoretes between the seventh and tenth centuries of the Common Era (CE)." "Masoretic Text," accessed October 22, 2020, https://en.wikipedia.org/wiki/Masoretic_Text.

Sardis was an extremely prosperous city. The city's elite enjoyed congregating in prominent locations with each other and with those travelling in and out of the city. They talked about philosophy, commerce, culture, and probably faith, as their city was comprised of a variety of religions which got along well with one another. But despite its apparent prosperity, this church was doing something detestable in God's sight. Jesus told them to wake up and strengthen that which was about to die. There was a glimmer of hope that some in the Sardis church were not completely dead. Jesus had not totally given up on them; He told them to wake up before it was too late. There was hope, but the church needed to act quickly for it to revive and thrive again as His church.

Revelation 3:3

> *Remember, then, what you received and heard. Keep it, and repent. If you will not wake up, I will come like a thief, and you will not know at what hour I will come against you.*

This glimmer of hope is related to what the church had initially received, heard, and believed. Although their present works are incomplete, they had held to the truth, a small spark of which still smoldered. Sardis must fan the flames of that truth; repent of their wrongdoing; turn away from their overconfidence, compromise, self-sufficiency, and pride in self, others, and the world; wake up and turn from their sin; and revive what they had almost lost. This is their last opportunity. If they do not wake up and repent, they will be lost when Jesus comes against them.

Revelation 3:4–6

> *Yet you have still a few names in Sardis, people who have not soiled their garments, and they will walk with me in white, for they are worthy. The one who conquers will be clothed thus in white garments, and I will never blot his name out of the book of life. I will*

confess his name before my Father and before his
angels. He who has an ear, let him hear what the
Spirit says to the churches.

The few in Sardis with unsoiled garments, who had not capitulated to the world and sinned against God, will walk with Jesus in white: they are the worthy victors, the overcomers, Christians who stayed the course and whose names are written in the Lamb's book of life (Rev. 21:27). They will spend eternity with God. That the names of these conquerors are left in the book of life may lead some to infer that the names of those who turn from God and never repent could have their names removed from that book. The clause "and I will never blot his name out of the book of life" is sometimes used to debate the once-saved-always-saved doctrine. If names can be removed but are not, the salvation of those professing to be "Christian," but who continue in sin and do not repent, is not secure. They may not be Christians.

Jesus will confess the names of those in white, the conquerors, before God and His angels. There was hope for some in Sardis, but those who were self-sufficient and falling asleep, who thought that they were safe when they were not, must wake up or be lost. Sardis thought it was safe at least twice before but was conquered because of its hubris. We do not know how long the church of Sardis kept its lampstand, but it had at least one faithful believer: Bishop Melito, in the second century.

Putting the Pieces Together

Today Sardis could be ranked as one of the ten best places to live. It had a low crime rate and its citizens were financially well off. Sardis epitomized peace on earth, but it did not endure faithfully. It had laid itself bare to attack.

Christians are to be in relationship with God first, while being loving and truthful to everyone. Living such a life is only possible when the Holy Spirit guards and directs every thought, word, and action. Most Christians in Sardis had become nominal Christians, their spirits dulled by worldly ways and their faith compromised to the extent that they no longer put God first. They loved their lives, loved the world, and, most disconcerting of all, pleased the devil. They were doing things the way of Sardis—the way of the world—and promoted this way of living. They had shut their ears to God. If they had heard or read Paul's letter to the Romans, they did not heed it:

> I appeal to you therefore, brothers, by the mercies of God, to present your bodies as a living sacrifice, holy and acceptable to God, which is your spiritual worship. Do not be conformed to this world, but be transformed by the renewal of your mind, that by testing you may discern what is the will of God, what is good and acceptable and perfect. (Rom. 12:1–2)

It is impossible to be a Christian and straddle two worlds or serve two masters. *Impossible.* Straddling causes the body extreme discomfort, if not disjointedness. Any person who serves two masters is double-minded, sometimes two-faced, and, also, often may speak with a forked tongue. Their loyalty to God is split and their thinking, actions, and words show it. It is not uncommon for Christians to be in compromising situations or in circumstances where they must choose to live that moment outside of Christian values, ignoring beliefs, and not speaking against what is wrong. But by taking a stand against God and what He says is right and not vigorously defending Christian faith and values, one's salvation is compromised.

The Bible is the greatest gift to humanity; it provides nourishment for the soul. Asa, king of Judah for forty-one years (c.913–910 to 873–869 BC), faithfully battled rampant idolatry for thirty-five years but became worldly, refusing to listen to the seer, Hanani, and rely on God. The king became angry and, when stricken with a foot disease, did not seek God: "In the thirty-ninth year of his reign Asa was diseased in his feet, and his disease became severe. Yet even in his disease he did not seek the LORD but sought help from physicians"

(2 Chron. 16:12). King Asa's sin was not that he consulted physicians but that he did so apart from God.

Today people are growing increasingly angry and bitter with God, with Christians, and with the Bible, because God does not conform to what they wish Him to be. Like the other churches, the church in Sardis probably understood the ramifications of its letter, but ignored its message. Instead, it accommodated the world, and, therefore, it did not survive long.

Promoting Sin: Of the World

In Sardis, a city of comfort and compromise, most were affluent and happy with the status quo. Although God calls us to live peacefully together and to love our neighbors, we must never deny Him. The belief that all religions are the same, with everyone going to heaven (or nirvana, or wherever) as they pass from this world or incarnation to the next, was as popular in first-century Sardis as it is today, but it is antithetical to the Bible. Jesus says that He alone is the way to God (John 14:6; Acts 16:31). Christians know that they cannot follow Jesus and universalism (the doctrine that everyone is going to heaven), because His words describe the opposite.

What happened in Sardis is an excellent example of what has always happened throughout history. As Christians work to get along with others, they often compromise Christian beliefs in order to be accepted. Eventually churches select and dilute the Bible and doctrine that they teach so that everyone feels comfortable. The attributes of a supposedly loving God are debated and parts of the Bible that are regarded as hateful and unloving are either denied or reinterpreted rather than being discussed. Following an exclusive Jesus is wrongly considered a denial of any possibility of living together peacefully. Accepting everyone's beliefs as equally valid truths is promoted. Beliefs and worship styles are not merely discussed but borrowed, assimilated, and over time accepted and then promoted. Living as the Sardis church members did went beyond tolerance and love for other people and past respectfully disagreeing with another's faith. It grew into acceptance and promotion of other beliefs as equal to their own.

What the Sardis church believed had become a combination of scriptural teachings, commonly held secular beliefs, and imported ideas. In this way, no religion was deemed better than the next. A merging of beliefs allowed people to discuss philosophical ideas, socialize at the gymnasium, shop in the stores, and attend each other's religious gatherings as one family. Over time, this resulted in unity of all thoughts and ideas, even spiritual ones. Christians, like the Jews, were no longer true to God first. Everyone placed their faith in God after family, community life, and friends, united in their beliefs with people of other religions.

Syncretism, then, is a problem throughout the Bible, for both Israel and the early Christians. The Israelites had the mistaken idea that they had to agree with others in order to love and live with them, especially in marriages with foreign women. Ahab and Jezebel, and Solomon with his thousand wives, princesses, and concubines, illustrate this.[78] Syncretism is the result of misunderstood and misplaced love and loyalty.

The Bible is clear: Christians are different from non-Christians. Not just made in God's image, Christians are the adopted children of their Father, God. Christians do not love the other if they compromise God's truth and promote other religions contrary to Him. In addition to missing an opportunity to testify of God and His love, they jeopardize their own salvation. When Christians disagree with friends and family, they must not reject God and His ways but honestly, lovingly, and patiently explain the reasons for their disagreement.

---

[78] Read about Ahab in 1 Kings 16:29–33; 18:1–4; 21:1–29, and about Solomon's wives in 1 Kings 11.

Living Life in a Syncretic World

Not being *of* the world is not what people think that it is. Putting God in first place and everything and everyone else, including the self, after Him, results from what God does in Christians' hearts. If Christians are to love and pray for their enemies, they must do the same for family and friends. They must love them enough to reason with them, explain who God is, and why they believe what they believe. When God is first on your mind and in your heart in the morning and the last in the evening, living out of God's love comes as a gift of grace through the Holy Spirit. Christians understand then how they are related to God and an integral part of His family.

Although some indicate that they have and/or want a personal relationship with God, knowing Him is impossible without prayer, Bible study, and Christian fellowship. Omit any one of these and one is prey to one's own body, the world, and the devil. There is a monumental difference between calling oneself a Christian and being one. A Christian is a new creation in Christ, transformed for all to see.

The battle that Christians are engaged in today is like that of the first-century Sardis Christians. They may recall some Bible verses and teaching but have been lured by the devil through others, corrupted by the world's ways, and lulled into complacency. Many are hard-working with "kind" hearts who wish to feed the hungry, clothe and house the poor, and empathize with the hurting, but are misguided into thinking and believing that what the world believes is better than God, His Word, and His ways. "If it feels good do it; you are not hurting anyone," a common mantra, is doublemindedness and sin against God, and it affects each unrepentant sinner for eternity.

Many who call themselves Christians today are syncretists. They are generous, loving people who promote all religions, values, and opinions. While Christians must protect the rights of all people to make their own choices, they cannot promote all religions, values, and opinions. The world is confused—embroiled in controversy over who God is, what He approves of, and what He hates. Church members choose what sin is most distasteful and grievous in their eyes without consulting the Bible or their leaders or without praying. One Christian is pitted against another regarding what the Bible deems to be sin: pagan influences (e.g., Easter, Halloween, Christmas, yoga), sexuality (e.g., pre-marital sex is fine if pregnancy and STDs are avoided, etc.), and other topics. Some churches avoid any offence or controversy by refusing to define and discuss sexual sin (e.g., adultery, fornication, sodomy).

The world we live in has a different agenda from God's and that of Christians. Because of poor counsel from friends and family, and with few ties or affiliation to a Bible-centered Christian community, most people can hardly be expected to be anything else but of the world. Except for prayer. Christians pray for their family, friends, strangers, and even enemies. They pray especially for those that they love who are living apart from God. Everyone needs prayer, but praying for the lost is the one thing Christians know that they can do, because "more things are wrought by prayer than this world dreams of: Wherefore, let thy voice, rise like a fountain ... night and day."[79]

Prayer increases faith. It is uplifting to watch people change as the Holy Spirit works in their lives. Changed lives are everywhere: in hospitals, prisons, universities, and churches. Numerous stories of conversion can be read, watched on social media, or listened to on radio, blog, or vlog.[80] Countless lives have been changed and will continue to change from sin and despair to boldly proclaiming the love of God.

---

[79] Alfred Lord Tennyson, *Idylls of the King* (London: MacMillan and Co. Limited, 1899).

[80] The internet is a tool for learning and a living source of Christian hope. David Arthur, George Carneal, Charlene Cothran, Becket Cook, and Joe Dallas turned from sexual immorality to Christ. Dr. Kathi Aultman, Dr. Grazie Christie, Abby Johnson, Dr. Noreen Johnson, and Dr. Anthony Levatino used to agree with and perform abortions but now lobby for the rights of the unborn. These stories of love and transformation, and many more, are available on YouTube.

Sardis in Our Time

Today, we live in a beyond-Sardis-like era. Many people are not interested in hearing about other religions, ideologies, or opposing viewpoints. More and more, the "loving" world of the late twentieth century unites in shunning, ridiculing, and hating Christians because they are angry with, or hate, God Himself. Love, a popular buzzword of the past, is often replaced by the word *spirituality*. Many profess to be "spiritual," but there are many spirits. Some of these spirits are evil and life-taking. People need to know which spirits are being discussed. The devil uses everything and everyone to compete against God for His created souls.

When Christians think of the intricacy and needs of their own bodies, they often contemplate God and the awe and complexity of the universe that He created. God knows every being, every system, and every galaxy because He fashioned them to work together. Many people think that they have life all figured out until something goes wrong. Our ability to explore and discover God's vast creation and His laws governing that creation show that we are merely scratching the surface.

Some who call themselves Christians today live affluent lifestyles but give little time to the God who made them. Instead of giving God the firstfruits of their lives, He is given any leftovers, if anything. Others honestly struggle to remain faithful to God in a world that continuously pushes the limits. They pray for the world, the church, those they love—and themselves.

Antinomianism, one of the worst sins, is the belief that once people are saved by the blood of Christ they can live as they wish to live under His grace. This is a gross misrepresentation of Christianity. Christians know that they must not live a sinful life.[81] Jesus did not come to abolish the law but to fulfill it. He prayed to His Father to be kept from temptation and sin. Acquiescing to fleshly desires can lead to every imaginable sin. Christians know that sin is an abomination

---

[81] The author of the letter to the Hebrews explains this error well. See Hebrews 10:26–39.

to God and destroys people. They avoid it, but repent after every sin they commit, because they know what God detests.

Christians who live in faithful communities are fortunate for they have support in guarding their minds and hearts in order not to be drawn into heresy. Rooted and grounded in faith, they have fellowship with other Christians, which includes sound Bible study that helps them fight false doctrine. Non-Western Christians are more often financially poor and persecuted for their beliefs, but they treasure and study the few Bible portions that they have; they are abundantly rich, because they know the Lord.

Unless humans fill their spiritual void with God, they find other means of satisfying and quenching it. When they are threatened with problems, sudden illness or death, floods, hurricanes, earthquakes, or viral pandemics, they need more of those substances to which they are addicted in order to cope. The emotionally stressed lament: "If it weren't for my (cigarettes, alcohol, drugs—whatever crutches used to help), I just couldn't cope." Other unhealthy and worldly means of coping with stress include gambling, pornography, sex, materialism, overeating, and social media. The list is long, but whatever preoccupies the mind to remove stress is often a barrier to God, the only one who can help people deal with their stress and be fully alive.

In this addicted world, it is often easier to compromise and do as the majority do rather than to stand against their sin. Some governments promote more of what the Bible calls sin, as it continues to decriminalize more substances and behaviors, while, at the same time, taking greater control of people. The overall standard of living has improved, but nations that were affluent fifty years ago are less so today. More people are surprised by how rapidly much of the world is uniting on popular left-leaning views regarding population, climate, and mind control. Revelation implicitly warns of mighty shifts that will occur as standards of living decline and lawlessness increases.[82]

---

[82] "Everyone who makes a practice of sinning also practices lawlessness; sin is lawlessness. You know that he appeared to take away sins, and in him there is no sin. No one who abides in him keeps on sinning; no one who keeps on sinning

When we put our trust in ability, intelligence, money, material possessions, and worldly (often sexual) love, we may feel satisfaction but lose our souls as quickly as we lose our lives. Except for the love of God, all is lost. When we trust God to regenerate us and work through us, we become worthy witnesses and holy instruments for God's use, as Paul was after his conversion. As Jesus told Paul:

> But rise and stand upon your feet, for I have appeared to you for this purpose, to appoint you as a servant and witness to the things in which you have seen me and to those in which I will appear to you, delivering you from your people and from the Gentiles—to whom I am sending you to open their eyes, so they may turn from darkness to light and from the power of Satan to God, that they may receive forgiveness of sins and a place among those who are sanctified by faith in me. (Acts 26:16–18)

We know from the letter to their church that there were faithful Christians in Sardis in the first century. There were probably Christians in all seven churches who persevered to serve God by conquering the devil, their own flesh, and the world through patiently enduring in the power of the Holy Spirit. Christians have always been encouraged by the overcomers that Jesus describes in Revelation. They know what is expected and where to find the strength that they need to overcome and endure.

Like the early church, all who are called to witness and teach the gospel must do what God requires in love, truth, and humility. Gently but confidently, they uphold the Bible but avoid hateful talk and

---

has either seen him or known him. Little children, let no one deceive you. Whoever practices righteousness is righteous, as he is righteous. Whoever makes a practice of sinning is of the devil, for the devil has been sinning from the beginning. The reason the Son of God appeared was to destroy the works of the devil. No one born of God makes a practice of sinning, for God's seed abides in him, and he cannot keep on sinning because he has been born of God. By this it is evident who are the children of God, and who are the children of the devil; whoever does not practice righteousness is not of God, nor is the one who does not love his brother" (1 John 3:4–10).

arguments. Christians pray for God's guidance to help them be the most-loving Christian examples that they can be for family, friends, and strangers. Their security is in Jesus, and they clothe themselves in God's full armor (Gal. 6:10–20) to avoid being drawn astray by the self, the devil, or the world. Without the Bible and prayer, it is easy to think that one is serving God, when actually one is serving oneself, the devil, and the world. All too soon, life is over, and the world goes on without you—while you have all eternity to pay.

Christian church at the rear of the temple to Artemis, Sardis.

Section VI

In Truth with Love

So we have come to know and to believe the love that God has for us. God is love, and whoever abides in love abides in God, and God abides in him. By this is love perfected with us, so that we may have confidence for the day of judgment, because as he is so also are we in this world. There is no fear in love, but perfect love casts out fear. For fear has to do with punishment, and whoever fears has not been perfected in love. We love because he first loved us. (1 John 4:16–19)

Remains of the sixth- century Byzantine Church of Saint John,
Alaşehir, Turkey, home of what was ancient Philadelphia,
the second of two faithful churches of Revelation.

CHAPTER 8

Philadelphia—Faithful Love

And to the angel of the church in Philadelphia write: "The words of the holy one, the true one, who has the key of David, who opens and no one will shut, who shuts and no one opens.

"I know your works. Behold, I have set before you an open door, which no one is able to shut. I know that you have but little power, and yet you have kept my word and have not denied my name. Behold, I will make those of the synagogue of Satan who say that they are Jews and are not, but lie—behold, I will make them come and bow down before your feet, and they will learn that I have loved you. Because you have kept my word about patient endurance, I will keep you from the hour of trial that is coming on the whole world, to try those who dwell on the earth. I am coming soon. Hold fast what you have, so that no one may seize your crown. The one who conquers, I will make him a pillar in the temple of my God. Never shall he go out of it, and I will write on him the name of my God, and the name of the city of my God, the new Jerusalem, which comes down from my God out of heaven, and my own new name. He who has an ear, let him hear what the Spirit says to the churches." (Rev. 3:7–13)

Philadelphia, the second of the seven churches given no rebuke, is also not threatened with consequences for disobedience, because it has been obedient. One of the last churches to be planted—probably by John—it became known as the loving church. John wrote about God's love and goodness in his gospel and letters. He cared for Jesus's mother until she died, lived a godly life while founding churches in Asia Minor, and endured persecution well into old age. John served the church for about thirty years after both Peter and Paul were martyred. The first-century churches in Asia Minor knew John and his teachings. He was no doubt talked about long after his death.

Where in the World Is Philadelphia?

Philadelphia is located about twenty-eight miles southeast of Sardis. Its ancient remains lie within Alaşehir, a town in the district of Manisa province in the Aegean region of Turkey in the Kuzuçay Valley at the foot of the Bozdağ Mountain, Mount Tmolus in antiquity. Alaşehir is approximately eighty miles east of Smyrna and about sixty miles northwest of Laodicea.

History and Archaeology

Philadelphia was a popular name for a city in antiquity, but the Philadelphia housing the sixth church of Revelation was one of the first ancient cities by that name. In 189 BC, King Eumenes II of Pergamum established Philadelphos, meaning "one who loves his brother," in honor of his brother nicknamed Philadelphos because of his loyalty to King Eumenes. Philadelphos succeeded Eumenes II, as Attalus II.

Attalus III, the last of the Attalid kings of Pergamum, bequeathed his kingdom to his Roman allies when he died in 133 BC. When the province of Asia was established by Rome in 129 BC, Ionia and the former kingdom of Pergamum were combined. Greek culture and language quickly spread from Philadelphia due to the city's strategic location at the intersection of Mysia, Lydia, and Phrygia, its junction with one important highway linking the east to the west, and another diagonal route coming from Pergamum. Known for its many gods, pagan temples, architecture, and beautiful buildings, it was called Little Athens.[83] Philadelphia was renowned for its grape vineyards due to rich fertile volcanic soil, and it was the center of worship for the Greek god Dionysius, the god of wine.

Earthquakes made Philadelphia a dangerous city. The Roman emperor Tiberius gave the city financial relief by waiving taxes after earthquake damage in 17 AD. The city subsequently honored Tiberius. Unearthed coins reveal that Caligula also helped the city. Under Caligula's leadership, Philadelphia housed an imperial cult. Not much remains of ancient or Roman Philadelphia except a small theater on the northern edge of Toptepe Hill.

In the sixth century AD, Philadelphia was a prosperous Byzantine city, but it was not entirely converted to Christianity, as there were still festivals and temples to pagan gods. The domed Basilica of St. John, built around 600 AD, provides the remains that most tourists visit at Alaşehir. However, the Byzantine walls once surrounding the city have crumbled. In the late eleventh century, the Seljuk Turks conquered Philadelphia, but during the First Crusade, in 1098 AD, it was recovered by Byzantine emperor Alexios I. It was the center of several revolts against Byzantine emperors in the twelfth and thirteenth centuries. The city was made the metropolis of Lydia in the fourteenth century by the Greek Orthodox patriarch of Constantinople because it resisted the Ottomans. Philadelphia prospered as an important producer of leather goods and red dyed silk in the thirteenth and fourteenth centuries.

In 1922, Alaşehir was destroyed by fire. It had been occupied during the Greco-Turkish war of 1919 to 1922 by the Greek army but no one is sure if the fire was caused by the Greeks or the Turks. About three thousand lost their lives. A suburb in Athens, Greece, is named after Greek refugees from Alaşehir settling there after the war.

---

[83] "Philadelphia: The Seven Churches of Revelation," accessed March 13, 2018, www.biblestudy.org/biblepic/churches-of-revelation-philadelphia.html.

Christianity had a prominent presence in Philadelphia, especially within the Orthodox and Roman Catholic churches.

Inwardly Digesting Revelation 3:7–13

Revelation 3:7

And to the angel of the church in Philadelphia write: The words of the holy one, the true one, who has the key of David, who opens and no one will shut, who shuts and no one opens.

This message to the church in Philadelphia is from the holy and true one who has the key of David, Jesus Himself. Philadelphia was a temple warden, like Athens, and gave its emperor the title "the son of the holy one."[84] This may be why Jesus is called "the holy one, the true one" in His message, but this does not detract from the fact that Jesus is God; Roman emperors and pagan gods are not. The Philadelphia church knew this. It lived triumphantly and victoriously through Christ for God in the first century AD. What a great assurance it was for Christians in Philadelphia to know that Jesus was with them spiritually. Faithful to its Lord and Savior, the church there knew that Jesus opens doors no one will shut and closes doors no one will open. If the Lord is with you, who can be against you?

Revelation 3:8

I know your works. Behold, I have set before you an open door, which no one is able to shut. I know that you have but little power, and yet you have kept my word and have not denied my name.

---

[84] "Philadelphia Seven Churches of Revelation," accessed January 31, 2020, https://autumnridgechurch.wordpress.com/philadelphia/1/31/2020.

Jesus had opened a door for the church in Philadelphia because it preached the truth and spread the gospel with love. No one could close that door, as worldly power was inconsequential. Because it was faithful, this church was given supernatural strength to do God's will. Although it had little worldly power, because its members were financially poor with no political clout, the Philadelphian church refused to compromise its faith. It was spiritually empowered to proclaim Jesus even in the toughest circumstances. This church's assurance through Christ outweighed all worldly power and prestige.

Revelation 3:9

> *Behold I will make those of the synagogue of Satan who say that they are Jews and are not, but lie—behold, I will make them come and bow down before your feet and they will learn that I have loved you.*

Although the church in Philadelphia likely grew out of the Jewish community there, at the time of this letter Christians and Jews were not getting along. Jesus associated those of the synagogue with Satan. He harshly rebukes these Jews, calling them liars. Either in their lives or after their deaths, Jesus says that He will make the Philadelphian Jews cower before the Christians and learn who God's Son is. Jesus loved the church in Philadelphia because of its faithfulness, perseverance, and suffering. To those in pain, Jesus's love is more precious than the greatest human love. The Christians of Philadelphia knew Jesus's love and passed it on. Out of their godly love, some Jews may have come to know Jesus through them. A faithful church like this one makes a noticeable difference to everyone with whom it comes in contact.

Revelation 3:10

> *Because you have kept my word about patient endurance, I will keep you from the hour of trial that is coming on the whole world, to try those who dwell on the earth.*

Those who treasure Jesus as their most-precious gift often find it easier to be patient, as they cherish this pearl of great price (Matt. 13:46). The Philadelphia church had likely been reminded of the importance of patient endurance. Jesus tells them that because of their faithful, patient endurance He would keep them from the hour of trial that was going to come on the whole world to test it.

Those who trust Jesus know that God is omnipotent. They are assured that all things will work together for their good. This is what resting in the Lord means. This verse is sometimes used to support a pre-tribulation rapture that some believe happens with Revelation 4:1. They believe that the faithful will be removed before the world undergoes the tribulation described in Matthew 24, Mark 13, Luke 21, and Revelation.

Revelation 3:11

> *I am coming soon. Hold fast what you have, so that*
> *no one may seize your crown.*

This is the first of four times that Jesus says that He is coming soon. All four phrases are in Revelation (22:7, 12, 20). The short sentence "I am coming soon" must have reassured the Philadelphians. Jesus would come in the twinkling of an eye (1 Cor. 15:52). They could not know the exact time, but it was crucial that they be ready. The church in Philadelphia heard. It was enduring, awake, ready, and discerning. We do not know what they endured, but with temple worship, religious games and festivals, and Jewish abuse, they likely considered that the earthquakes were minor in comparison.

Jesus entreats them to stay the course so that no one would take their crowns. Faithful Philadelphians would receive an unspecified crown. The only other faithful church, Smyrna, was promised the Crown of Life (Rev. 2:10). The Christians of Philadelphia might receive one of five heavenly crowns: the crown of glory (1 Pet. 5:4), imperishability or incorruptibility (1 Cor. 9:25), righteousness (2 Tim. 4:8), rejoicing (1 Thess. 2:19; Phil. 4:1), life (James 1:12; Rev. 2:10), or an unidentified one. Their crowns would not perish like the olive branch crown given to Olympic champions.

For two millennia, Christians have sought the meaning of the words "Jesus is coming soon." Prayers for Jesus to come soon are bittersweet for Christians because they know that when He does return many will be lost. The Philadelphia church may have put greater effort into reaching the lost and praying more fervently and more often because of this promise. It may have prayed without ceasing.

Revelation 3:12–13

> *The one who conquers, I will make him a pillar in the temple of my God. Never shall he go out of it, and I will write on him the name of my God, and the name of the city of my God, the new Jerusalem, which comes down from my God out of heaven, and my own new name. He who has an ear, let him hear what the Spirit says to the churches.*

Jesus again refers to the conquerors, those who will be with Him in heaven. Being made into a pillar in the temple of God probably held special meaning for Philadelphian Christians: their city contained temples, and earthquakes were a constant threat. Often temples were destroyed, with only one or two pillars remaining. Pillars are usually the most significant parts of a building, supporting it from foundation to roof. Jesus praised the Christians in Philadelphia when He told them that they were like standing pillars in God's temple. They were foundational to God and His church. The phrase "never shall he go out of it" held special meaning for this church because many of its members regularly moved to huts outside the city in the open country when earthquake threats came, and returned when the earthquake was over.[85]

Large pillars bearing different markings have been excavated throughout Turkey. In Laodicea, one pillar shows a palm branch

---

[85] Ibid.

(or lulav), a ram's horn (or shofar), and a menorah, all of which are Jewish symbols, followed by a Christian cross.

Those who heard the letter to Philadelphia were reassured. The church would keep its lampstand because those serving in it patiently and faithfully endured in Christ. These Christians knew what to do because they desired to serve God. They loved God as He loved them. It was with this love that they loved others.

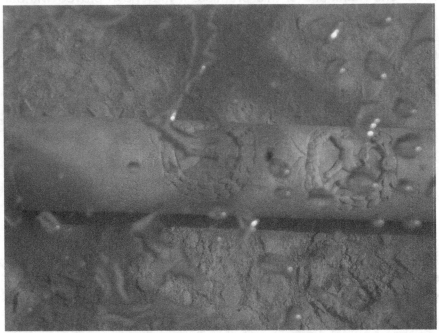

Ancient pillar with markings, underneath a glass floor in Laodicea.

Putting the Pieces Together

The Philadelphian church was wise and discerned God's will. Jesus tells church members that, because they have not denied His name, He will summon the Jews to bow down before them and they will learn how Jesus loves His followers (v. 9).

We live in a Bible famine, and it is, therefore, exceedingly difficult to know what is true, loving, and of God. Sometimes what is right and good is presented as evil, and what is wrong as good and loving. We can only be sure of our faith and that we are in God's will through a real relationship with Him and by believing the Bible. The hope of poverty-stricken Christians who are persecuted is that the new kingdom Jesus ushers in will not include pain or persecution. There Christians will worship God in love and truth without fear of reprisal. Jesus is the way to God—the source of eternal life—the joy of heaven. He is the living water and the bread of life. Jesus directed His apostles to continue, after His death, the communal breaking of bread in remembrance of His body, all that He is, all that He did for humanity, and all that Christians will eternally enjoy.

Fresh bread in a bakery window near the
Byzantine church ruins, Alaşehir.

Just outside the sixth-century Byzantine Church of St. John in Alaşehir, modern-day Philadelphia, a bakery displaying fresh bread in its window reminds Christian tourists of the Bread of Life. In the first of John's teachings of Jesus's *I Am* statements (John 6:35), Jesus says: "I am the bread of life; whoever comes to me shall not hunger, and whoever believes in me shall never thirst." Jesus teaches that we must eat His flesh and drink His blood in order to be in His Kingdom. Whether this is metaphorical or a literal statement is a controversial issue that loving Christians do not get caught up in. God alone knows. Breaking bread with other Christians as Jesus instituted is meaningful and powerful.[86] Metaphorically eating the Word of God satisfies spiritual hunger. The seventh and last of Jesus's *I Am* statements (John 15:1–12) has much to teach of spiritual nourishment and God's deep love for His children.

Jesus Is the True Vine

I am the true vine, and my Father is the vinedresser. Every branch in me that does not bear fruit he takes away, and every branch that does bear fruit he prunes, that it may bear more fruit. Already you are clean because of the word that I have spoken to you. Abide in me, and I in you. As the branch cannot bear fruit by itself, unless it abides in the vine, neither can you, unless you abide in me. I am the vine; you are the branches. Whoever abides in me and I in him, he it is that bears much fruit, for apart from me you can do nothing. If anyone does not abide in me he is thrown away like a branch and withers; and the branches are gathered, thrown into the fire, and burned. If you abide in me, and my words abide in you, ask whatever you wish, and it will be done for you. By this my Father is glorified, that you may bear much fruit and so prove to be my disciples. As the Father has loved me, so have I loved you. Abide in my love. If you keep my commandments, you will abide in my love, just as I have kept my Father's commandments and abide in his love. These things I have spoken to you, that my

---

[86] Erin Blakemore, "Buzz Aldrin Took Holy Communion on the Moon: NASA Kept It Quiet," accessed January 23, 2021, https://www.history.com/news/buzz-aldrin-communion-apollo-11-nasa#:~:text=Part%20of%20his%20mission%20was,prepare%20for%20their%20moon%20walk. Buzz Aldrin, a Presbyterian at the time, had lunar communion on the moon's Sea of Tranquility, as Neil Armstrong, the first man to step on the moon, quietly watched during their moon walk on July 20,1969. See Matt. 26:17–29; Mark 14:12–25; Luke 22:7–23; 1 Cor. 11:23–26.

joy may be in you, and that your joy may be full. This is my commandment, that you love one another as I have loved you. (John 15:1–12)

John 15, one of the richest chapters of the Bible, describes Jesus's relationship with His Father. Jesus tells Christians that they must have the same dependency on Him as He has on God. If not, they are dead, not *of* Him, and their works are useless; they cannot produce good and loving works if they do not know Him. People can only know godly love by receiving it from God, reciprocating it, and passing it on to others. They can only know goodness when they follow God and teach the goodness that He is. Their relationship with God and each other should mirror God's love for His Son.

The Greek language has four words for love: *agape, eros, phileo*, and *storge*. The Philadelphian church was named for phileo love, the brotherly, friendly, or affectionate love. This is not the love spoken of in John 15 or in most of John's writings. Eros, referring to romantic love and perhaps the most-common understanding of love in our times, is not mentioned in the New Testament. Storge, used a few times in the Bible, is also related to familial love, but it is not the love of John 15.

John was an expert on God's love. In John 15, he speaks of agape love. God expects this type of love from us, as we love others with the love of which John speaks. Agape, a rare Greek word, represents the highest and most noble form of love. It is the saving love of Jesus, the love of grace. The church in Philadelphia taught the truth with godly agape love, not the municipal phileo love of their city. This church knew the love of the Father, and its members loved other people—even those who had persecuted them—with that same priceless love that Jesus gave them. This is the love that draws people to God, forgiving them, and healing them to have true freedom in Christ.

Loving Others in Truth as God Does

You cannot love others with godly love if you do not first love God. Those who love God through Christ become Christ-like, new persons in Him. They are enabled by the Holy Spirit to sit beside those who are hurting and sinning, because they know that this is where they once were, and would still be, without Jesus. Christians follow Christ and obey God's commandments even when it is unpopular and difficult to do. They repent whenever they sin. This process of sanctification continues until death.

Paul, in Galatians 5:22–23, places love at the top of the list of the fruits of the spirit: love, joy, peace, patience, kindness, goodness, faithfulness, gentleness, and self-control. Godly love is honest and sincere to the point of giving up one's own desire of an easy life, dying to self, dying for friends, and perhaps dying for enemies. True love does not hide the truth or relish deceit, but it is gentle. This love comes from a changed heart.

A changed heart happens when Jesus comes into a person's life. Some have Damascus Road transformations like Paul did, because of God's agape love for them. Far more common than dramatic conversions are the slow and steady change in hearts.[87] We cannot predict how God will call or whom He may use, if anyone, to transform a life, but whatever He does, He does because He loves greatly. Christians are called to have agape love so that they can witness passionately to every person with whom they connect because they love them and want them to have eternal life. They know that the "unrighteous will not inherit the kingdom of God" (1 Cor. 6:9). Christians want to be God's vessels.

---

[87] Sophia Lee, "Freedom for the Same Sex Attracted," https://world.wng. org/2015/09/freedom_for_the_same_sex_attracted 2/21/2020. Becket Cook became a Christian September 20, 2009. He lived a life he knew to be contrary to what God and the Bible teaches is the life of a follower of Jesus Christ. An affluent, openly gay Hollywood production designer with an empty space inside of him, Becket had a conversion experience while attending Reality L. A. evangelical church. After his conversion, Becket attended seminary and in July 2019 published *A Change of Affection: A Gay Man's Incredible Story of Redemption*. His testimony can be viewed on YouTube.

Some "Christians" cherry-pick Bible passages, omitting portions they deem less loving, because they do not want to offend anyone. Christians, however, know that they must present the gospel fully and honestly so that non-Christians are convicted by the Holy Spirit to love God and His ways. God's faithful servants are directed by the Holy Spirit to lovingly use whatever God chooses to soften and transform human hearts, not purposefully leaving out any portions of the Bible. Being told that God loves you so much that He sent Jesus to wash you free of sin so that you can speak directly to a holy God impacts many hearts. With remorseful, repentant hearts, many speak freely to God and seek strength to turn from their sins.

Christians do not fully love others if they are not completely honest with them. They look to Jesus, the Bible, and prayer for the Holy Spirit to inform and provide strength for them to love everyone in complete truth. The only way that they can resist the temptation to let dishonesty slip by is through the power of God. Christians love God's ways. They do not want to dishonor Him, because they love Him and know how precious salvation is; they honor the family unit of man, woman, and children based in God's love of relating. The God-ordained family represents the wholeness that will occur when Jesus reunites with His bride, the church. Those who want to relate with God follow His ways as the Philadelphian church did. They want to be within God's will and do not want to revert to sinful lifestyles. When sin occurs, it is repented of and forgiven.

When Christians love others with agape love, they pray, often silently, for those who are lost in sin. After developing a relationship with non-Christians, Christians do not hide what the Bible says. What loving person hides life-saving information from anyone? What Christian wants anyone to wallow in sin and heartache? Rather than ignore biblical passages that describe sin, church leaders must teach about sin and its consequences (worldly and spiritual) and how to overcome it through the grace of God.

Those overcoming any type of sin through faith in Christ and in the power of the Holy Spirit no longer live a life of the flesh as they once did; as branches of the True Vine, they walk by the Spirit within them.

As children of God and conquerors, they will receive crowns of victory. Crowns went only to two faithful churches: Smyrna and Philadelphia (Rev. 2:10; 3:11), but all faithful Christians will receive crowns.

Philadelphia in Our Time

The letter to Philadelphia has much to teach the world but few want to read the Bible and obey God, because the world does not love God. This does not stop the God of perfect love from calling and redeeming His beloved, those who accept His love.

Humanity was marred by sin from the beginning. It had to be because in order to truly love God there must be an option not to love Him. Faith enables Christians not only to obey God but also to want to choose God's will over their own. Abraham, Moses, David, and Jesus's siblings were broken and sinful people like us, but God used them mightily. Christians today sense an increasing urgency to spread God's Word. They know that when God opens a door for someone to love Him, no one can shut it.

Passion and zeal for Christ and the Bible is spread by the Holy Spirit out of God's love. When people see the light of Christ for the first time and believe in Him, their transformation begins. Many come to faith through underground networks of Christians, through personal prayer and reflection, and via social media and other platforms. If a door closes, God has allowed or caused it to be closed, but He can open a new one. Christians are everywhere. The many different avenues that God uses for Christians to gather and commune with Him, sing, and study the Bible could only come through His miraculous love. Christians worldwide are spiritually united in God's love.

The Philadelphian church is the opposite of the Ephesian church. Doing many things right and having everything it could hope for, the church in Ephesus had nothing, because it had lost its first love. Having extraordinarily little, the church in Philadelphia had the bread of life, spiritual nourishment that prepared them for spiritual battle. It had no worldly power, but it opened and shut doors in Jesus's name.

The Philadelphian church chose to follow Christ, patiently enduring to the end because they had proper spiritual nourishment. They withstood being unpopular, poor, disadvantaged, and ostracized for their beliefs because their first love was God and they knew Him. We, too, must be faithful to God's call and know Him so that we may endure pain, hurtful comments, and criticism from family, friends, and others. God sustains Christians with His grace as they come to understand that they do not expect others to accept what they believe. They do not want non-Christians to accept *their* word; it is God's Word—God who is speaking, not them. Speaking God's love in truth with the courage of conviction is the ultimate love anyone can have for another person.

Christians are nourished spiritually by Jesus, the Bread of Life, and the Bible, the Word of Life, to live fully each day to and for God's glory; all else is vanity and a striving after the wind (Eccl. 1:14b). Those who have a relationship with God rejoice in living for Him, knowing that they will have eternal life. God's love, goodness, truth, and grace are more than sufficient.

The church of Philadelphia had an unobstructed view of God. Christians there loved His voice, knew His ways, and loved as He does. They were patiently faithful and knew that their eternal lives were secure through Jesus. Christians like those in Philadelphia and Smyrna know that they need a Savior. They see the door that Jesus has opened for them and know that no one can shut it for they are eternally victorious through Him. They do not negate or downplay sin, repentance, and forgiveness; nor do they add to, remove, or reinterpret portions of the Bible. Rather they welcome God's refining power through the Holy Spirit. They want everyone to know and love Jesus as they love Him.

The more we allow the Holy Spirit to remove our sin and turn our hearts toward God, away from the worldly things we once loved and thought pleasurable, but which are against God and muddy our view of Him, the freer we are to see and enjoy God's marvels. His character becomes vivid, and we relate to Him more deeply because we can spiritually see Him better. As we do, we begin to enjoy and desire what God does, not what the world does. We want to be better children, more like His Son.

An ancient olive press in Hierapolis, Turkey.[88]

For I want you to know how great a struggle I have
for you and for those at Laodicea and for all who
have not seen me face to face, that their hearts may
be encouraged, being knit together in love, to reach
all the riches of full assurance of understanding and
the knowledge of God's mystery, which is Christ, in
whom are hidden all the treasures of wisdom and
knowledge. I say this in order that no one may delude
you with plausible arguments. (Col. 2:1–4)

---

[88] "Unearthed—Rome's Gate to Hell (Hierapolis)," November 25, 2020,
Ancient History Nerd, accessed December 2, 2020, www.youtube.com/
watch?v=HTQZreirbew. Laodicea's sister city of Hierapolis is about six miles
north of Laodicea. It is well known for its large Necropolis (city of the dead), hot
springs, and huge white calcium deposits, whose water was used to dye textiles
in Pamukkale (Turkish for cotton castle). Founded by Greeks, Rome took over
Hierapolis in 133 BC. Hierapolis (meaning holy or sacred city) was a thriving city
of twelve thousand, with gymnasiums, popular temples, and amphitheatres. It was
well known for Pluto's Cave or Plutonium, a shrine to Pluto. First-century BC Greek
historian Strabo wrote of its entrance to the underworld.

Section VII

Lost

To the pure, all things are pure, but to the defiled and unbelieving, nothing is pure; but both their minds and their consciences are defiled. They profess to know God, but they deny him by their works. They are detestable, disobedient, unfit for any good work. (Titus 1:15–16)

Archaeological ruins of ancient Laodicea, Turkey.

For you say, I am rich, I have prospered, and I need nothing, not realizing that you are wretched, pitiable, poor, blind, and naked. I counsel you to buy from me gold refined by fire, so that you may be rich, and white garments so that you may clothe yourself and the shame of your nakedness may not be seen, and salve to anoint your eyes, so that you may see. Those whom I love, I reprove and discipline, so be zealous and repent. Behold, I stand at the door and knock. If anyone hears my voice and opens the door, I will come in to him and eat with him, and he with me. (Rev. 3:17–20)

CHAPTER 9

Laodicea—Hopelessly Lost

And to the angel of the church in Laodicea write: "The words of the Amen, the faithful and true witness, the beginning of God's creation.

"I know your works: you are neither cold nor hot. Would that you were either cold or hot! So, because you are lukewarm, and neither hot nor cold, I will spit you out of my mouth. For you say, I am rich, I have prospered, and I need nothing, not realizing that you are wretched, pitiable, poor, blind, and naked. I counsel you to buy from me gold refined by fire, so that you may be rich, and white garments so that you may clothe yourself and the shame of your nakedness may not be seen, and salve to anoint your eyes, so that you may see. Those whom I love, I reprove and discipline, so be zealous and repent. Behold, I stand at the door and knock. If anyone hears my voice and opens the door, I will come in to him and eat with him, and he with me. The one who conquers, I will grant him to sit with me on my throne, as I also conquered and sat down with my Father on his throne. He who has an ear, let him hear what the Spirit says to the churches." (Rev. 3:14–22)

Laodicea, or Laodikeia, on the Lycus River, was a thriving Roman metropolis of the province of Phrygia in Asia. At the time of the writing of Revelation, it was positioned on a natural trade route. As the last letter written to the seven churches of Revelation, the letter to the church of Laodicea has extraordinary meaning. It represents the church at its worst, with no soul, and as it may be upon Jesus's second coming.

Where in the World Is Laodicea?

Ancient Laodicea is located within the province of Denizli in Turkey near the city of Denizli, which is surrounded by many ancient cities, including the biblical Hierapolis and Colossae both of which are important to understanding the Laodicean church and other churches in its vicinity.

Laodicea lies about sixty miles southeast of Philadelphia (Alaşehir) and almost one hundred miles east of Ephesus. The archaeological site of ancient Laodicea was placed on the Tentative List of World Heritage Sites on April 15, 2013. The sprawling collection of ruins and artifacts is approximately eleven miles north of the unexcavated mound of Colossae and just over six miles south of Hierapolis/Pamukkale.

History and Archaeology

Laodicea was originally the Hellenistic Diospolis, City of Zeus, but was later called Rhodas. Antiochus II Theos is attributed with building the city in 261–253 BC in honor of his wife, Laodice.[89] Laodicea's checkered past swung between prominence and prosperity into oppression and back into prosperity again. It prospered under its first emperors. After oppression by the Roman Empire and the Mithridatic Wars, it rebounded and became a flourishing commercial site in Asia Minor. Its clothing and textile industries used goat's wool with a distinctive black color due to minerals in the goats' drinking water.

As Laodicea grew, it became a wealthy banking and exchange center. One account tells how, in 62 BC, Flaccus, proconsul of Asia,

---

[89] "Laodicea on the Lycus," accessed June 1, 2018, https://en.wikipedia.org/wiki/Laodicea_on_the_Lycus.

impounded twenty pounds of gold that the Laodicean Jews had sent to Jerusalem.[90] Twenty pounds of gold in that day was worth a tremendous amount. Laodicea minted coins with images of Zeus, Asclepius, Apollo, and Roman emperors printed on them from the second century BC.

Over time, Laodicea accumulated all the amenities of a large city: an agora, a stadium, temples, baths, a gymnasium, large Hellenistic and Roman theaters, a senate house, colonnaded streets, and a water tower and running water via aqueducts. The city boasted a prominent school of ophthalmology which developed a salve made from *collyrium* spices, which was applied like a poultice to treat affected ears and eyes.[91]

Although it was commonly thought that water was brought to Laodicea from Hierapolis in the north, a marble slab dated 114 AD unearthed in 2015 in Laodicea outlined strict laws regarding the water brought through channels from the Karci mountains over fifteen miles to the south.[92] Greek inscriptions on the slab describe ancient water laws that involved penalties from 5,000 to 12,500 denarius.[93] Regardless of its source, by the time the precious water reached the city, it was lukewarm. Large pipes and other artifacts excavated in Laodicea reveal that it was an engineering marvel.

Christianity in Laodicea began as early as 50 AD within the Jewish community. A bishopric formed early on indicates that it was a strong church. Paul's letter to the Colossians, written around 62 AD, sent with Tychicus and Onesimus for delivery at the same time as his letters to the Ephesians and Philemon, mentioned that he was concerned about Laodicea, but he was unable to visit them at that time.

---

[90] "Who Are the Laodiceans?" accessed February 22, 2020, https://www.ucg/bible-study-tools/bible-questions-and-answers/who-are-the-laodiceans.
[91] Ibid.
[92] "Ancient 'water law' Unearthed in Laodicea," accessed June 1, 2018, https://www.hurriyetdailynews.com/ancient-water-law-unearthed-in-laodicea--87259.
[93] In 2021, 125,000 Turkish lira equals approximately US$15,000.

Paul warned Christians to put to death whatever was worldly in them: sexual immorality, impurity, passion, evil desire, and covetousness, which is idolatry (Col. 3:5–6). Because of such sins, the wrath of God would come upon them. In verse 11, he encouraged them: "there is neither Greek nor Jew, circumcised, or uncircumcised, Barbarian, Scythian, slave, or free but Christ is all and in all." Greetings were sent from Epaphras of Colossae, who worked hard for Phrygian Christians in Colossae, Laodicea, and Hierapolis. Paul told the churches to share their letters with each other, as they experienced similar issues.

The Council of Laodicea (363–364 AD), a regional synod of approximately thirty clerics from Asia Minor, addressed the conduct of church members, especially judaizing (practicing Jewish customs and traditions). It instituted 59th and 60th canons regarding the biblical canon, and it condemned astrology. The 59th canon forbade the reading of uncanonical books in church. The 60th canon, listing twenty-six canonical books for the New Testament, omitted Revelation. This canon is in dispute because it is not in some Greek manuscripts. It may have been added to uphold the preceding 59th canon.[94]

Throughout its history, like many towns and cities in the vicinity, Laodicea was plagued by earthquakes. Eventually, after particularly severe earthquakes in the fifth and sixth centuries, the city was abandoned.

Inwardly Digesting Revelation 3:14–22

Revelation 3:14

> *And to the angel of the church in Laodicea write: The words of the Amen, the faithful and true witness, the beginning of God's creation.*

---

[94] "Council of Laodicea," accessed February 23, 2020, https://wikipedia.org/wiki/Council_of_Laodicea.

Jesus ensured that the Laodicean church knew who was speaking to them. He, the Lord Jesus Christ, not only witnessed creation but He created the heavens and the earth. He is bringing truth to them in ratification from God, the Father.

Jesus, the Amen, the beginning and the end, is truth. *Amen* means "so be it" in a formal sense in the Old and New Testaments; it implies certainty. All that is spoken is of the Lord. Amen, used to close prayer, signifies that others agree with what has been said. Jesus, the Word made flesh, is the beginning and the end. Laodicea's letter, the final letter for the churches in Revelation, also has a final message for the world today.

Water pipes lying on the ground in Laodicea, Turkey.

Revelation 3:15

I know your works: you are neither cold nor hot.
Would that you were either cold or hot!

This is an unequivocal rebuke. Jesus's reference to its works as being neither hot nor cold, like their own water, informed the Laodiceans that the problem in their church was serious. Their running water, although the result of an engineering feat, was unfit to drink. It was equally disgusting for washing and bathing. The works of the Laodicean church were neither cold nor hot and served no purpose, just as the water being pumped into their houses. This church now knew that whatever they were doing as a church was useless.

Revelation 3:16

> So, because you are lukewarm, and neither hot nor cold, I will spit you out of my mouth.

For the works of the church to be compared to Laodicea's lukewarm water meant that their actions were a waste of time. Jesus's words must have made their hearts sink: Jesus wanted nothing to do with their works or their church. If their works had been either cold or hot, they would have indicated purpose and hope. If they had been wrong in how they did their works, it might have been possible for them to have been corrected and redirected. Being lukewarm meant that the Laodicean church had no heart or passion. As it gave only lip service to being a church, it would have been better for it never to have existed.

Revelation 3:17

> For you say, I am rich, I have prospered, and I need nothing, not realizing that you are wretched, pitiable, poor, blind, and naked.

The comfortable, self-sufficient Laodiceans were pitiful in their prosperity; although they had the best clothing, food, entertainment, and medical care, they could not see and they did not know what they lacked. That Laodicea was known for its perfect eye salve made

Jesus's message more poignant. Jesus said that they were naked and did not realize that they were naked, unlike Adam and Eve after the fall, which placed them in worse shape spiritually. This church had done the work of Christ's church terribly. It could treat hearing and sight and clothe their nakedness, but spiritually they were deaf, blind, and naked.

Jesus tells them that what they think and say is false. The truth: the church in Laodicea was wretched, pitiable, poor, blind, and naked. Even though they had the finest clothing, they were not clothed in the righteousness of Christ's blood. They were to be more pitied than those who were poor, blind, and deaf. The Laodiceans desired only pleasant drinking water, but according to Jesus they had nothing. Spiritually, they are destitute: they do not have the living water of Jesus Christ, that pure life-giving water that takes away all thirst and cleanses from all sin.

Revelation 3:18

> *I counsel you to buy from me gold refined by fire, so that you may be rich, and white garments so that you may clothe yourself and the shame of your nakedness may not be seen, and salve to anoint your eyes, so that you may see.*

Despite the poor prognosis, Jesus offers the Laodicean church godly counsel: to heed His words. Although this church is spiritually poor and blind, there is hope. It needs the gold of faith—refinement by His fire to have its spiritual nakedness covered in white to gain spiritual sight. Gold represents the divine. The person who has faith in Christ has gold that no one can steal. Gold refined by fire has been tested and sealed by the blood of Christ and by the Holy Spirit. This spiritual gold changes and refines those who buy (take or accept) it so that they have everything they need in the Lord Jesus Christ.

Compared to the wardrobes of the Laodiceans, which were probably mostly black, Christ tells them to clothe themselves in white garments that are washed clean and pure, which represent the holiness and worthiness of Christ. Clothed in black represents being clothed in darkness; white represents purity, the light of Christ and the love of God.

Lastly, Jesus refers to sight, something which made many Laodiceans proud of their famous city's cure for blindness. People came from all over to buy its eye salve. Many in the church could not understand Jesus's message, probably because they were preoccupied with living busy, happy, materialistic, and self-fulfilling lives. They did not need Christ. In worldly terms, the Laodicean church was wealthy, but it did not know or see what was spiritually most important. Would it hear, understand, spiritually see, and act on Jesus's wise counsel before it was too late? Would they ever understand that the greatest love in life does not come from this life or this world but is of God?

Revelation 3:19

> *Those whom I love, I reprove and discipline, so be zealous and repent.*

Jesus tells the Laodiceans that He loves them. Despite their waywardness, He wants them to return to Him. He disciplines them and gives them the opportunity to repent, as He did with the other sinful churches. If this church were half as zealous about faith in and love for Jesus as it was about community, resources, wealth, and an opulent lifestyle, its members would have listened and opened their eyes. They would have repented and returned to Jesus as their first love.

Revelation 3:20

> *Behold, I stand at the door and knock. If anyone hears my voice and opens the door, I will come in to him and eat with him and he with me.*

Jesus pleads for His lost sheep. He wants each one to return to the fold. He knocks and waits patiently and lovingly for them to return. He did this for those in the Laodicean church. This church needed a softened heart to hear Jesus's voice and answer His call. But the church had lost its senses. Jesus alone knows who, if anyone at all, from the church of Laodicea believed in Him and accepted His gift of eternal life before it was too late. Although this church may have been lost, individual Christians within it may have known Jesus and were saved.

Revelation 3:21–22

> *The one who conquers, I will grant him to sit with me on my throne, as I also conquered and sat down with my Father on his throne. He who has an ear, let him hear what the Spirit says to the churches.*

Jesus pleads for each person to be an overcomer as He was, to live eternally with Him. Everyone can become right with God, although all have sinned and fallen short of His glory. Because Jesus intercedes when Christians sin and repent, they are forgiven through His work. God will not coerce anyone to believe. Every person must make a choice and live with the consequences of that choice for eternity.

Putting the Pieces Together

Jesus leaves the worst for last. The Laodicean church exemplifies the purposelessness of a prosperous life and the senselessness of a sensual life apart from God. One may have the whole world but lose one's soul. Laodicea had everything except wholesome drinking water—and eternal life. This church shows how easy it is to have everything of the world while being eternally lost.

Human life can only be sustained for three minutes without oxygen but for three days without water. Laodicea's water, although it was potable, was foul. Compared to the hot springs to the north in Hierapolis and Pamukkule, Laodicea's lukewarm water was unsuitable for bathing or therapeutic use. Compared to the cold water of Colossae, it was unwholesome. Laodiceans had the best of everything, but its church, like its drinking water, was disgusting and useless.

Ironically, the church in Laodicea was the opposite of the churches in Smyrna and Philadelphia, who had little materially but were rich in faith. Christians in Smyrna had good drinking water, but both Smyrna and Philadelphia Christians drank freely of the living water of Jesus Christ. Laodicea did not fully understand that Jesus is the only source of perfect living water that can quench thirst.

Like its water, the Laodicean church was not fulfilling its purpose. Although Ephesus had lost its first love, it was still trying to testify to God's goodness. Laodicea was self-sufficient and wealthy; it even had a salve that claimed to cure blindness, but it was wretched and spiritually blind. It did not have pleasant drinking water or hot bathing water, but throwing away the living water of Christ was egregious. It had no godly love, no right teaching, and no God-honoring works. It existed in name only.

The Laodicean church practised faith out of a sense of obligation. Its letter shows how following in someone's footsteps merely for the sake of following them is useless. The Old Testament Israelites may have felt that because they were born into God's chosen family, they had to keep up their faith traditions. Maybe they thought that because this was their birthright, they had few responsibilities outside of being Jewish. Although Jesus fulfilled God's plan of salvation as Messiah to the Jews first, many Jews did not accept Him.

The Laodicean church believed in Jesus as their Messiah at first, but in a short time it no longer loved and accepted Jesus above all else, as Smyrna and Philadelphia did. Paul's epistles to the Ephesians, the Colossians, and Philemon are helpful in contextualizing first-century Christian life in Asia Minor. The letters to Colossae and to Philemon particularly aid in understanding Jesus's message to the Laodicean church because life in Colossae was like life in Laodicea. The letter to the Colossians suggests that there was a letter to Laodicea, but it has not been found. Of the seven churches of Revelation, only a letter to Ephesus is included in the biblical canon; however, there is plenty in these seven letters for Christians to know what God expects of His church.

Colossae, Hierapolis (meaning holy or sacred city), and Laodicea had large Christian communities in the first century, but Christianity was not their main religion until the third to fourth centuries. All three of these churches overseen by Epaphras had serious spiritual and geological problems. Their spiritual issues sprang out of their being pagan, well-to-do Roman cities. Colossae, a grassy mound yet to be unearthed, was as important as Hierapolis, a World Heritage Site since 1988, and Laodicea until it lost its commercial status in the first century BC.[95] The church in Colossae was threatened by gnosticism, a widespread heresy in which adherents believed that they had secret knowledge. Delightful hot springs and huge travertines make Hierapolis and Pamukkale popular tourist destinations. Ancient ruins reveal the lavish lifestyle of the inhabitants and those who visited from the second century BC to the early centuries AD. Ancient Hierapolis, a healing medical center with natural hot mineral springs, was considered a demonic stronghold, with a hole going right through it to hell. Early Christians believed that they had overcome the problem when they filled the hole with rubble.[96] Colossae, Hierapolis, and Laodicea eventually succumbed to earthquakes.[97]

---

[95] David Padfield, "Colosse, Hierapolis and Laodicea," accessed February 1, 2020, https://www.padfield.com/2015/colosse-laodicea.html.
[96] Bob Cromwell, "Pamukkale, Hierapolis, and Laodicea, near Denizli, Turkey," accessed February 23, 2020, https://cromwell-intl.com/travel/turkey/pamukkale/.
[97] "Laodicea on the Lycus," accessed January 13, 2020, https://turkish archaeonews.net/site/Laodicea-lycus. Contrary information about Laodicea's demise exists. Documents for UNESCO World Heritage registration and Mark Wilson's *Biblical Archaeology* say that the city was abandoned after an earthquake during the reign of emperor Phocas (602–610), and the residents moved to the city of Denizli. Byzantine writers, however, often wrote of Laodicea, especially during the reign of the Komnenos dynasty, in the eleventh and twelfth centuries. Byzantine historian Niketas Choniates said that the city was repeatedly plundered

According to scientific information about earthquake formation and probability, the center of the earth is said to be about the same temperature as the sun. The early Christians believed in hell (pit, fiery furnace, or Sheol), but today many dismiss it despite the approximate 100 Bible verses that affirm its existence. Jesus said that those who receive the mark of the beast will go to hell (Rev. 14:9–11). Many ridicule hell and the devil but the Bible says both are real (Matt. 13:15; 25:41; Mark 9:43; Rev. 20:10; 21:8).

The Laodicean church did not understand why Jesus lived and died. It is clear why the fourth-century council voted the book of Revelation out of the canon. Why would they include a book that condemned five of seven churches to hell if they did not repent and change, especially when the worst one was their own?

Senseless, Hopeless, and Lost

The church in Laodicea, known for its prosperity and its famous eye salve, was itself blind and deaf metaphorically. It had hardened its heart against God's Word. According to John's letter, it had little, if any, biblical understanding. Jesus taught that anyone who followed fleshly desires, earthly conveniences, and an evil master would not experience worldly contentment or have eternal life. This led the Laodicean church to be forever lost. If only they had heeded Paul's earlier letter to the Colossian church:

> Therefore, as you received Christ Jesus the Lord, so walk in him, rooted and built up in him and established in the faith, just as you were taught, abounding in thanksgiving. See to it that no one takes you captive by philosophy and empty deceit, according to human tradition, according to the elemental spirits of the world and not according to Christ. (Col. 2:6–8)

---

by the Turks and the Mongols and that the last inhabitants left in the thirteenth century.

The Laodicean church trusted in human efforts. Its members worshipped the efforts of their own hands rather than thanking God for everything. They did not walk like Jesus walked but were taken captive by the world: money, financial expertise, and deceit. They had succumbed to sins of the flesh, the world, and the devil.

Paul wrote letters to the Colossians, Ephesians, Philippians, and Philemon (the prison epistles) between 60 and 62 AD. He responded to their respective situations and encouraged them to grow in Christian maturity. He told the Colossians to ensure that the Laodiceans also read the letter, but if they had, they did not heed his instructions. The church in Laodicea gained the whole world but lost its soul. It should have heard the gospels, but like many lost churches today, it may not have been exposed to them. If it had, it would have heard Jesus's words: "For what does it profit a man to gain the whole world and forfeit his soul?" (Mark 8:36).[98] This was not a new spiritual concept. Jesus taught from the Hebrew Scripture, for example: "For he sees that even the wise die; the fool and the stupid alike must perish and leave their wealth to others" (Ps. 49:10).[99]

The church in Laodicea was lost. It had not wisely used its God-given gifts of sense, intelligence, or love. No amount of beauty, money, or medicine would help them. They did not heed the Hebrew Scripture, Christian epistles, or their Revelation letter.

Laodicea in Our Time

People today live what they believe to be fulfilling lives, filled with busyness as the Laodiceans did, but with technological devices and every convenience. They want life their way, with everything they need and want, much of it outside of God's laws and will. They do not want a God whose thoughts and ways contradict theirs, who has

---

[98] See also Matthew 16:26, "For what will it profit a man if he gains the whole world and forfeits its soul? Or what shall a man give in return for his soul?"
[99] See Job 27:8–23, Luke 12:13–21, and Psalm 49, which tells why Christians do not need to fear anything.

authority over them, and who makes demands on them. Many do not acknowledge God, much less follow His ways. Comfortable in their affluence, they live in the moment with little thought of what will happen when life is over. Some Christians are uncomfortable talking about God even with other Christians. The God of the Bible has been dismissed, de-mythologized like the underworld gods in Hierapolis, and replaced by gods of affluence, imagination, narcissism, and worldly power but who have no substance.

Many say that they care about relationships, relationship building, and recovering from broken relationships, but few seem willing to do any hard, soul-searching work to change themselves. Even fewer care about relating to God because most living in this Laodicean-like world do not see any need for a relationship with God. They depend on and praise themselves, individually and corporately, just as the Laodiceans did. Many prefer less personal communication. They are less able to critically analyze with any unbiased depth of understanding. Far less value is placed on directly talking with others than even a decade ago, as many text those who are sitting beside them. Credit for this techno-savvy world goes to the powerful and wealthy with agendas of their own.

People place great importance on dexterity; most ever mindful of the gadgets in their pockets or on their desks. Fewer people have time for strangers (much less God), yet meaningless texts and posts interrupt meetings, meals, and other people's time. God is often blamed for what is wrong but given little credit when things go well. More hesitate to give God public credit or glory for His creation or the gifts He has given them, as people themselves are credited with improving life. Giving God credit is considered weak, superstitious, or ignorant. When an enemy is defeated, it is praised as the strength and wisdom of competent people uniting to fight a common enemy. Few thank God publicly and fewer still exhibit concern for others. All of this grieves God's heart, as the core message and purpose of the Bible is to reach others in love for Christ.

In stark contrast to the church of Laodicea are the faithful churches of Smyrna and Philadelphia. The extremely poor church of Smyrna had little except Christ, and because of Christ, they were persecuted. The church in Philadelphia had little power, but it worked powerfully in love for God. Christians in both churches were guaranteed Holy Spirit power and eternity with Christ. Likewise today faithful Christians throughout the world empowered by the Holy Spirit love and serve others with God's love and truth.

Those faithfully and patiently enduring for Christ spread the good news to what is largely an idolatrous, pagan world like Laodicea was. Prophecy is being fulfilled, as life for Christians increasingly worsens: "lawlessness will be increased, the love of many will grow cold. But the one who endures to the end will be saved" (Matt. 24:12–13). Jesus's revelation in concordance with the entire Bible has and continues to buoy up and build up Christ's body to battle darkness with that love which never grows cold.

Dark Days: Not of God's Love and Goodness

The early church was warned to take no part in the unfruitful works of darkness but to expose them (Eph. 5:11). The church in Laodicea did not obey God. If it could explain why it did not repent and change, it may have blamed its water or earthquakes. But there are no valid excuses to snub or ignore God. Tragic circumstances may cause people to reflect on the meaning of life. This may be an excuse to stay away from God or the impetus to draw closer. Sometimes trust in and support of government leaders cause some to seek something more profound. Other times inconsistent rules, coupled with hypocrisy, cause backlash, some of which may be aimed at churches.

In recent decades, backlash over hypocrisy and unrepented hidden sin within churches and church leadership has caused much disillusionment and member exodus. Everything is questioned and not much respected in our present age. Disrespect for religious institutions is understandable, but transferring the sins of humanity to the God of Judaism and Christianity, which results in persecution and violence, is not.

The institutional church has not done a proper job of living and teaching the Bible. It has not exposed the evil that threatens or harms people physically, emotionally, or spiritually. When the church does not teach and uphold God's truth yet allows culture to obfuscate the Bible, much confusion ensues. When Jesus returns, all people will know truth. There will be a reckoning, especially for church leaders. Christians have nothing to fear, as their salvation is contingent on believing in Jesus, not on following church leaders.

Christians today too often accept and believe the words of those who profess to be Christian, yet who do not believe in Jesus or the Bible. Some appear to be wise and loving, as they promote self-made religion, but they are easily exposed when they are tested against the Bible. Imposters do not know God, His love, His truth, or His will. They cannot help the lost. What started in Laodicea with people being lulled into complacency deteriorated into an age of ego, greed, self-entitlement, and corruption.

Poor definitions and poorly delineated lines create confusion and inroads for those facets of society which wish to jettison Christianity, while increasingly respecting other religions in order to fulfill their goals. Delegitimizing Christianity diminishes it and results in greater problems and more pervasive needs. The one true and holy God will not be dethroned. According to Revelation, evil will end. In the meantime, Christians must be as wise as serpents and innocent as doves.

Wisdom and discernment are paramount to Christianity. But wisdom often has multiple facets. Not only is there a far right and a far left, but there are multiple far rights and far lefts, with many varying their stance on issues so that they can be a combination of far right and far left when it is expedient. Christian leaders are under scrutiny, which is appropriate, but hatred of Christians makes for a difficult time for the church—but not unexpected for those who know the Bible. The world cannot have godly wisdom and discernment, just as it cannot have godly love; it is in for darker days ahead if it continues to be oblivious to its creator.

Everything good is of God. As the world, the devil, and our bodies tempt us, an increasingly tangled web of evil—misinformation, disinformation, and conspiracy theories—creates confusion. The nonsensical is given airtime and writing space at the expense of God's truth, goodness, and love. Although Christians sometimes deviate from Jesus's teachings, they love God first and want to uphold His ways. Scripture says that God will rescue the godly (2 Pet. 2:9). Christians know that money and power, not godly love and truth, are at the center of most dishonesty.

As the world's view of God becomes increasingly vague, some courageous Christians will speak out more. They will experience greater persecution and be called to make difficult choices. Christian discernment will become increasingly important as greater numbers of false teachers vie for hearts, minds, and souls. Some Christians may be deceived but God will provide strength for those who repent.

The church has always existed in a delicate balance. Some Christians blatantly cover up sin, including abuse, covetousness, greed, hatred, and murder, all against God and His will. Some sin, however, is deeply rooted and influenced by demons. The devil uses tools like segregation, discrimination, and mind and population control to attract megalomaniacs to work for him and further his lies. There is no perfect church in the world, but churches must deal with all sin, especially their own, some of which was done in the name of Christianity. Christians must unearth it and deal with it, as Jesus will, when He returns. This is the only way for the Christian remnant, those true to God, to grow more Christ-like. Much of the world is lost, as Laodicea was. The only hope for anyone is faith in Jesus.

Many people today have an emptiness they cannot fill. Increasingly more are depressed, weighed down by the world, and taking their own lives. God knows: "Anxiety in a man's heart weighs him down, but a good word makes him glad" (Prov. 12:25).

Faith in Jesus can address everything, even depression. Like those in Laodicea, many Christians today want for nothing. Some, creating god in their image, rant heresies publicly.[100] Some prefer no god: Greek, Roman, or the one true God of the Bible. Some are pagan without knowing it. The world tries to liberate itself from dependence on anything other than itself and encourages everyone to fulfill their dreams and determine what they are. Not only have many lost their love for God but they have released all hold on His truth.

Some Christians may look as if they are members of Christ's Church, but Jesus knows those who are His. They may be likened to a ripe, delicate peach that is beautiful and tempting on the outside, but with a worm deep in its pit, destroying it from the inside out. If the heart is not right with God, a person can have a happy, fulfilling, worldly life but be spiritually dead. Some may not know the extent of their depravity until they have died.

Days have often been dark for the church but, as Christ's return approaches, Christians will be pressured more and more to bend to their flesh, the world, and the devil. Jesus's words in Revelation must be studied in the context of the whole Bible to gain knowledge of what it means to be a Christian who patiently endures and is victorious in their faith, because many are being led astray.

Jesus's message is a warning. It must not be diluted through fleshly, worldly love of living, heretical or hermeneutical arguments, charismatic false teachers, or covered up by smooth loving liberality or progressivism. People must wake up and see what is ultimately important: they alone choose their path. One is life-giving, the other is deadly.[101]

Jesus's message is reassuring and comforting to Christians.

---

[100] Transition Studios' *American Gospel Christ Alone* (2018) and *Christ Crucified* (2020) have fascinating and shocking accounts of what some "Christians" deem to be Christian belief and doctrine.

[101] God will not allow sin to destroy His creation. As seen by Adam and Eve's expulsion from the garden due to disobedience (Gen. 3), Cain's curse due to murder and lies (Gen. 4:8–16), and Jesus's cursing the fig tree and overturning the tables in the temple (Mark 11:12–25), God's patience has a perfect limit.

The choice to love God, staying awake and enduring until the crown of life is victoriously given to all who walk with Christ in love, leads to heaven. Jesus pleads in His seven letters, as Paul and others do in the Bible, for everyone to wisely choose God through Him: to choose an earthly life that leads to eternal life. Not everyone will choose wisely.

Those who say "Yes" to Jesus form the biblical remnant of His church.

> Blessed are you when others revile you and persecute you and utter all kinds of evil against you falsely on my account. Rejoice and be glad, for your reward is great in heaven, for so they persecuted the prophets who were before you. (Matt. 5:11–12)

A cross on a Laodicean artifact (above) and a
medical symbol in Ephesus (below).

Section VIII

Heaven Bound—
The Faithful Hear

So at the present time there is a remnant, chosen by grace. (Rom. 11:5)

From inside the Smyrna site (above) and the Philadelphia site (below).

CHAPTER 10

Overcomers Hear, Endure, and Are Awake and Ready

> And all the churches will know that I am He who searches mind and heart, and I will give to each of you as your works deserve. (Rev. 2:23b)

God shows His love for humanity by ensuring that His Word endures. Ironically, as hatred for God and the Bible increase, more archaeological support for it comes to light. Revelation's seven letters describe the faithful remnant. Everyone could be part of this remnant but not everyone will choose to be. The world changes constantly but God and the Bible stay the same. Christians read it for wisdom and stand on its authority. They do not eliminate portions that they dislike, disagree with, do not understand, or are criticized. They add nothing to it but strive with God's help to live by it.

> These are the things that you shall do: speak the truth to one another; render in your gates judgments that are true and make for peace; do not devise evil in your hearts against one another, and love no false oath, for all these things I hate, declares the Lord. (Zech. 8:16–17)

The Biblical Remnant

The theme of a remnant is carried throughout the Bible and culminates in Revelation. With a decision to follow Jesus, Christians become children of God and part of His household. They are part of the biblical remnant that was begun in the Old Testament. The remnant learns and follows the Bible, although it is against their human nature.

Israel split into two kingdoms in 930 BC (2 Chron. 10). The Assyrians destroyed Israel in the north around 733–722 BC (2 Kgs. 17). Judah to the south, more faithful to God for a time, was defeated by Babylonian king Nebuchadnezzar. Jerusalem fell around 597-586 BC. Isaiah predicted that all this would happen:

> In that day the remnant of Israel and the survivors of the house of Jacob will no more lean on him who struck them, but will lean on the Lord, the Holy One of Israel, in truth. A remnant will return, the remnant of Jacob, to the mighty God. For though your people Israel be as the sand of the sea, only a remnant of them will return. Destruction is decreed, overflowing with righteousness. (Isa. 10:20–22)

The Jews, exiled to Babylon, were permitted to return to their ancestral homeland around 538 BC by a decree of King Cyrus of Persia, who overthrew the Babylonian king. They returned in three major groups, during which the scribe/priest Ezra was sent to teach them the Law of the Lord. Ezra confronted those returning with him around 458 BC about their intermarriage with idolatrous Gentiles. He led them to repentance and to separate from the Canaanites, Hittites, Perizzites, Jebusites, Ammonites, Moabites, Egyptians, and Amorites whom they had married:

> And after all that has come upon us for our evil deeds and for our great guilt, seeing that you, our God, have punished us less than our iniquities deserved and have given us such a remnant as this, shall we break

your commandments again and intermarry with the peoples who practice these abominations? Would you not be angry with us until you consumed us, so that there should be no remnant, nor any to escape? Oh Lord, the God of Israel, you are just, for we are left a remnant that has escaped, as it is today. Behold, we are before you in our guilt, for none can stand before you because of this. (Ezra 9:13–15)

Throughout their history, the Jewish people were unfaithful to God and failed to keep the Mosaic law. They believed in corporate salvation as God's chosen people, although individual faith was also important. Ezra told God, in the final part of his prayer, that the people did not deserve to be a remnant: they disobeyed by intermarrying with people who practiced abominations. He knew that God is righteous, just, merciful, and holy. God's mercy is evident in His permitting the Jews to return to their land. Because Ezra's prayer stirred some hearts to return to God, a remnant was preserved.

The fact that some of Israel was saved, as prophesied by Isaiah, testifies to God's bountiful love. Most of Israel was judged by the prophets to be in error. Only a remnant leaned on God and experienced salvation. Isaiah speaks of a patient trust in God during difficult times and urges listeners not to be drawn into pagan worship and occultism. Israel, he said, deserved to be wiped out like Sodom and Gomorrah, but God had spared a remnant. Israel fell repeatedly, but God continuously showed mercy. The New Testament reinforces what the prophets wrote about Israel's waywardness and the reason that God allowed them to be killed:

And Isaiah cries out concerning Israel: "Though the number of the sons of Israel be as the sand of the sea, only a remnant of them will be saved, for the Lord will carry out his sentence upon the earth fully and without delay." And as Isaiah predicted, "If the Lord of hosts had not left us offspring, we would have been like Sodom and become like Gomorrah." (Rom. 9:27–28)

God considers those loyal to Him as preservers of His Word. He speaks of weeding out the idolatrous, sexually immoral, and prideful, but preserving the faithful: "I will surely assemble all of you, O Jacob; I will gather the remnant of Israel; I will set them together like sheep in a fold, like a flock in its pasture, a noisy multitude of men" (Mic. 2:12).

God is perfectly merciful. He has always ensured the survival of His faithful people, but a remnant is not about numbers. It is about loyalty and obedience to God. God always hears those who sincerely call to Him, despite their inability to live a life worthy of Him. Those persecuted for their faith in Jesus are living testimonies of God's love. The remnant, although a result of God's judgment on His people, is also proof of His divine mercy on a group kept alive so that they would prosper with God's Word living in them. Ultimately, the remnant is unified through Jesus (Mic. 5:2–3).

The church, established by Christ in Jerusalem and spreading out into Judea, Samaria, Asia, Europe, and eventually the whole world, has changed drastically since its inception. What was the cradle of Christianity is all but decimated. What was paganism and idolatry in Jesus's day merely changed name and course. Idolatry of people, places, and things increase as the Bible continues to be dissected and grossly misinterpreted. The Bible (although sometimes used wrongly for power, control, and financial gain) is the anchor of the faithful remnant that holds firm to Jesus under the protection of the Holy Spirit. The seven letters of Revelation speak of and to this remnant but are relevant to anyone who reads or hears them. They contain warnings to heed and blessings to encourage amidst the call to salvation, obedience, and endurance until death, or Jesus returns.

Christ's church has suffered since its beginning. Christians answered the call and faithfully endured to spread the gospel. The author of *The Pilgrim's Progress*, first published in 1678, John Bunyan, preached faithfully to a Baptist congregation in Bedford, England, and the surrounding area from 1655 to 1660. Bunyan was not licensed to preach by the Church of England and was therefore imprisoned at the Bedford County Gaol, where he suffered in primitive conditions for twelve years, beginning in early 1661.[102] His famous book, said by some to be second only to the Bible, likely was written while he was incarcerated, with the Bible as his only reading material. Of his 369 biblical references, twenty-four come from Revelation: seven from chapters 2 and 3, and ten from chapters 21 and 22. Bunyan's complex theological allegory illustrates the good wrought through persecution, even when that persecution comes from Christians. Christianity has always spread through persecution. Through the suffering of people like Bunyan, who testified to their faith, others came to believe.

God's remnant seeks to please Him. Christians know that their survival is not due to any innate goodness, or any other person's, but solely to God's perfect goodness. Their living glorifies God: they love people as God loves them, because God's love shines through them as the Holy Spirit equips and guides them. Witnessing for God, they light a dark world that is passing away along with its desires. In doing the will of God, they abide forever (1 John 2:17).

The remnant is a disparate group of people who live all over the world, drawn together in their love, faith, and joy in Jesus and a desire to serve God through Him. They want to see Jesus and know God more through His Word. They do not believe that everyone goes to heaven, but only those known by Christ, who, on judgment day, will say "Yes, Father, I know this person and that person," will go there. The seven letters of Revelation reinforce this. Everyone could go to heaven, but not everyone will.

Those who love Jesus, and are known by their godly love for others, speak joy into life knowing that one day they will be reunited with all Christians in heaven. How this is so no one knows; such questions seek worldly answers to spiritual mysteries that defy human explanation or understanding. Trusting in Christ and knowing

---

[102] John Bunyan, *The Pilgrim's Progress: From This World to That Which Is to Come*, ed. C. J. Lovik (Wheaton, IL: Crossway, 2009), 11. Bunyan's book has drawn much attention and been made into several movies; an animated film was produced by Robert Fernandez in April 2019.

that He will return for His faithful bride one day are what matters most.

The Bride of Christ

> Then they gathered around him and asked him, "Lord, are you at this time going to restore the kingdom to Israel?"
>
> He said to them: "It is not for you to know the times or dates the Father has set by his own authority. But you will receive power when the Holy Spirit comes on you; and you will be my witnesses in Jerusalem, and in all Judea and Samaria, and to the ends of the earth." After he said this, he was taken up before their very eyes, and a cloud hid him from their sight.
>
> They were looking intently up into the sky as he was going, when suddenly two men dressed in white stood beside them. "Men of Galilee," they said, "why do you stand here looking into the sky? This same Jesus, who has been taken from you into heaven, will come back in the same way you have seen him go into heaven." (Acts 1:6–11 NIV)

Christ's ascent into heaven established His church. It was the end of His earthly journey with God's people and the beginning of His betrothal to the church. Comparing Jesus to a groom who will return for His bride, the church, parallels the Old Testament marriage analogy, wherein God, the loving husband of Israel, the unfaithful wife, patiently awaits for Israel to return to Him (Isa. 54:5; Jer. 31:32; Hos. 2:16).

When humanity was in perfect relationship and fellowship with God, the family unit was intact, as God had created it. Sin entered the world via Satan after creation. His reign is why humanity falls increasingly away from God, but Jesus defeated him, sin, and death at the cross. The world will increasingly fall further from God and His ways until Jesus returns for His faithful bride, at which time He will judge all people.

Standing Firmly on God's Love and Goodness in Truth

> But we ought always to give thanks to God for you,
> brothers beloved by the Lord, because God chose you
> as the firstfruits to be saved, through sanctification by
> the Spirit and belief in the truth. (2 Thess. 2:13)

The Bible is clear—everyone who knows God will be known by their love for God and His truth like the persecuted faithful of Thessalonica were known. But they may not be known for their righteousness, good works, or the love others feel that they should have. The first three verses of 1 Corinthians 13 state that if we do not have love, we are useless. We would be like Ephesus—teaching God's truth, hating evil, testing leaders, patiently enduring, maybe even giving away all that we own, but be lost. None of these will last, but God's agape selfless love will thrive forever. Because this pure love always radiates God's truth, it is often hated and rejected by the world. God's love does not rejoice in being right but in the eternal hope of His Word.

If Christians are to stand on God's truth, they must live it. They must know what is *of* the world in order to avoid it. Christians know that their disposition drives them to be selfish and pits one person against another. The world defines happiness, success, power, and "goodness" differently from how God does. Christians, who have a different worldview, define everything as God does, not as the world does.

In academia, facts are adhered to until proven false, but too often those with contrary rational ideas are not respected. Within theological scholarship as well, there is little respect for divergent thinkers. Those with differing viewpoints are often shunned, especially if someone is perceived as being exclusively loyal to the biblical God. Christians do not require tangible proof for their faith but archaeologists regularly unearth artifacts that unequivocally establish that the Bible has greater historical validity and reliability than formerly thought. Many choose to ignore these facts. It is irrational to invert the tenets of the Christian faith that were the basis of its establishment, and which have been supported by the Bible for about sixteen centuries, because of a few powerful people who have the will and the means to promote a worldly political agenda.

When scientists believe that all absolute truth rests in God alone, they are sometimes deemed "close-minded" and viewed as "pseudoscientists," even when they have open-mindedly studied everything about a topic, such as the beginning of the world.[103] They know that God strengthens them to stand firmly on His goodness and truth in love for their fellow scientists, regardless of beliefs. God equips them to stand in joy despite ridicule.

> Finally, be strong in the Lord and in the strength of his might. Put on the whole armor of God, that you may be able to stand against the schemes of the devil. For we do not wrestle against flesh and blood, but against the rulers, against the authorities, against the cosmic powers over this present darkness, against the spiritual forces of evil in the heavenly places. (Eph. 6:10–12)

Seven Warnings

The Bible is the ultimate plumbline. Revelation's visions, filled with cryptic images that mirror some Old Testament prophets' writings, help us understand what God wants us to know. If we are wise, we will heed its warnings. The following seven warnings are extrapolated from Jesus's revelation to the world through seven churches in first

---

[103] There are only two basic theories: creation and macroevolution. Well-educated, articulate scientists exist on both sides of the debate, yet some macroevolutionists choose to refer to creationists as "pseudoscientists" rather than admit that there are intricate questions much better addressed by young earth science than by macroevolution. See Dal Tackett's *Is Genesis History?* a 2017 documentary about creation. It is impossible to make an educated and rational choice in an unproveable matter without open-mindedly studying all viewpoints. A good debater will study and understand opposing viewpoints. Education is not indoctrination. There are numerous examples where science appears to contradict the Bible but there are also numerous counter arguments to these "contradictions."

century Asia Minor. They are relevant to Christians, to the church, and to the whole world.

1. You will be tempted by the world to be *of* it. *Do not be of the world.* EPHESUS.

We are social beings and like to be around others, but we are wise to think of the world's trappings—that which thrills and excites us, and are sinful—as fly paper. If we stick to it, the consequences are deadly. The church in Ephesus rooted out false teachers, false teaching, and false doctrine, but it did not love God first. Ephesus was not just in the world—it was of it. Christians must speak against false doctrine and false teaching, but it must be done in and with love for God first.

Christians must call on God when they are tempted to sin and be of the world. They do not "look like" or "look to" the world. The only way Christians are sure that they are not *of* the world is to keep their eyes and hearts looking to Jesus and walking in the power of His Spirit. They look heavenward to Jesus, love God first, and allow the Holy Spirit to move freely in them so that they can genuinely love others with God's love. God is the preeminent source of love and truth today as He was in the first century.

2. Christians will be persecuted for their faith in God. *Do not be afraid.* SMYRNA.

Just as the early Christians were persecuted for following Christ, Christians today will increasingly and more severely be persecuted for their faith. Christians must withstand governments that at best are neutral to all religions and at worst are openly anti-Christian. They live in communities where some calling themselves Christian are not. False gospels are worse than neutrality, idolatry, and atheism combined because they can look real and spiritually kill those with poor biblical understanding and little or no discernment.

The church in Smyrna, and Christians from the time of Christ, did not fear what could be done to their bodies. They knew that what was important could never be taken from them. Strengthened by the Holy Spirit, they withstood all that they had to bear. Christians in Smyrna knew that Jesus was with them through their trials and that they would receive eternal life for their faithfulness and patient endurance (Rev. 2:10). The Bible reassures us that God's perfect love casts out all fear. Jesus tells us to not be afraid, for He is always with us, even to the end of the age (Matt. 28:20). Second Timothy 1:7 reminds Christians that God has given them "a spirit not of fear but of power and love and self-control." Christians' lives are rarely easy, yet they learn to give thanks in all things. Some even give thanks in their persecution because they conquer evil "by the blood of the Lamb and by the word of their testimony, for they loved not their lives even unto death" (Rev. 12:11).

3. The devil will try to lure you into idolatry. *Know the enemy.* PERGAMUM.

First-century Christians had much to resist and fight in order to be faithful to God and avoid idolatry. They had to withstand the pressure to worship the pagan gods of Greece and Rome and the imperial cult of Rome. These Christians did not participate in the occult, astrology, witchcraft, or other diabolic temptations. They knew Scripture well enough to discern their enemies from those who were faithful. Protected by the Holy Spirit they were prepared to fight all that threatened them and their faith. Twenty-first-century idols include limitless materialism, narcissism, and hubris. Although first-century churches had access to Scripture, they did not have the ease of access as we do with one bound volume. The early church was not theologically adept as many claim to be today (albeit much is interwoven with false teaching) to help them understand the Bible but these Christians had unshakeable love for and trust in God.

After salvation, one's relationship with God deepens with prayer, Bible study, and fellowship with other Christians. Wisdom and discernment rather than human emotions and experiences are essential to fight the devil, his guises, tactics, and demons. The

Holy Spirit strengthens Christians to fight him regardless of how he presents himself. With hearts given to God and a love for the Bible, Christians are well equipped and Holy Spirit-led to know the enemy and to stand against his ploys.

4. Trials of the flesh will come. *Repent, and turn away from sin.* THYATIRA.

It is our bodies of flesh that we know best and which lure us into sin. It is human nature to want to feel comfortable, look good, and have pleasure. Our bodies, the devil, and the world tempt us to go against God at our points of least resistance. This may involve those we love, our associates, strangers, and enemies.

The Thyatiran church sinned against God. Associating with sinful people had resulted in an evil person coming into the church, gaining power, and influencing them to sin. Some chose Jezebel over Jesus, refused to turn from their wicked ways, and hence lost their souls. Poorly equipped to stand for Jesus, they fell, victims to sins of their flesh. We too fight Jezebel and other spirits. We must pray to resist the temptations to please our flesh. No special formula is required to talk to God. He knows when we are sincerely seeking Him. We must seek and talk with Him often about everything. Our relationship with Jesus and the Bible helps us to know sin, confess, repent, and be forgiven of it. When we choose Jesus, who was tempted and did not sin, He will help us find His way; we will regret and not repeat our sins.

Christians turn from sin and teach the truth in love to others. Welcoming people into the church does not mean that their sin is also welcome. Jesus always welcomed sinners, but He rooted out sin. The Bible defines sin and tells us how Jesus defeats it in repentant hearts. The Bible must be revered; God abhors compromise of His Word. Believing church leaders lead by godly example and are open and honest about sin, repentance, and forgiveness in Christ.

5. Things are often not as they appear. *Be awake, wary, and ready.* SARDIS.

The Sardis church looked alive, but it was dead. It enticed, but it had no integrity. What seems to be too good to be true often is. The seven letters show how looks can be deceiving. They are a stern warning for Christians to be awake and ready. What looks attractive may not be within God's will, while what looks unattractive or ugly may be wholesomely sound and of God's will. The world usually looks favorably on the superficial, but Jesus knows the depth of everyone's soul. He calls us to be wise and discerning, especially about the world we live in and the company we keep.

Smyrna and Philadelphia probably would not attract many to live there today just as they did not in the first century, but these two places held the only two churches that were faithful and which Jesus did not rebuke. Christians there discerned what was of the world, the devil, and the weaknesses of their flesh. They were victorious because they knew God's voice and knew what was of Him. They were awake, vigilant, and prepared to fight what was against God just as the faithful are today. Jesus warns the church to be prepared for whatever may come. In this way, it will be prepared for His return. No one knows the day or hour, but the Bible teaches the signs.

The churches in Smyrna and Philadelphia represent Christ's body. The other five churches—Ephesus, Pergamum, Thyatira, Sardis, and Laodicea—were prosperous, worldly places with many attractions. Their populations soared, as people flocked there to enjoy their amenities. Jesus was repulsed by their sin and their churches. The best friend anyone has, next to salvation through Jesus and the Holy Spirit inside them, is the Bible. Christians need this guidebook to discern what is of God. They beseech God for help in gaining godly discernment through Bible reading and prayer so that they are alert to the Holy Spirit's prompting of danger. Metaphorically, then, every Christian is awake in faith, is wary, and ready to stand guard against the devil and sin.

6. Human love can be deadly. Jesus saves. *Love and trust God first*. PHILADELPHIA.

We want the love of people until we experience the love of God. People need to be loved, but we are easily fooled. Our hearts are deceitful above all (Jer. 17:9). Only two of the seven churches knew God's love and could love as He did.

Human love, as much as it is desired, and as much as kind, loving people desire to help others, is not always of God. Consider the death toll caused by STDs; abortions; alcohol, drug, pornographic and gambling addictions; depression and suicide due to relationship breakdown; family breakdown; and emotional, physical, and sexual abuse. Sin within churches reaches beyond those who are physically, emotionally, and spiritually scarred by it at the hands of those who should have helped them. Such sin detracts from the perfect love of God because it assists the enemy. As a result, many who potentially may have found true, lasting relationship with God in a church did not. Unfortunately, too many are unable to differentiate between God and churches, in which people have attempted to institutionalize the divine. Much has been hidden and wrongly taught, but the guilty will be held accountable to God.

That space inside of us created solely for God's love is easily dulled by self-love and love of the world. Some determine that the best way to ensure being unhurt is to withdraw from society. Others guard their hearts by giving them to Jesus, trusting Him to be ever-present. Godliness flows from God's heart, but much evil flows from the human heart. The love with which people love impacts who they are, everything they do, and everyone they meet. Christians love others as God loves them, as the churches in Smyrna and Philadelphia did. They do not rely on the world's love, because they know that it is flawed. Christ's church is totally honest in teaching the truth of the gospel in love.

7. The world thwarts God's call. *Hold fast; faithfully and patiently endure.* LAODICEA.

The adage "you may be your own worst enemy" is true even with respect to Christians. Everyone is born with a sinful nature. The devil does not want anyone to know Jesus and he will do anything to draw attention away from Him. Our encounters with people and our experiences hinder our response to God's call to be faithful to Him because God and His ways are warped and misrepresented by the world. One of the devil's greatest tools is confusion. We need only consider popular "Christian" celebrations that divert attention from God. Jesus is not mentioned, hardly missed, as many absent-mindedly take His name in vain.

The Holy Spirit within Christians guards them from being fooled. Their prayers are often their first response to others' attempts to draw them away from God, but the Holy Spirit may inform a Christian to leave a situation or to contact a fellow believer. Learning how Jesus avoided temptation by prayer and reading and quoting Scripture strengthens Christians to fight what may threaten their faith or seduce them to sin. They become familiar with God's voice by reading the Bible and praying for safety. The Holy Spirit quickens their hearts to discern what is trustworthy. Avoiding people may not be necessary, but knowing whom and what must be fought helps Christians stand firm.

It is vital for Christians to know God so that they know what is not of Him and can take appropriate measures against their soul's enemies. Jesus calls them to guard their hearts, their minds, their time, and their resources against the busyness of the world, which fights relationship with God through Him. Christians pray for strength, comfort, and guidance to stand firm in faith, holding fast to God's promises to never leave them or forsake them.

Revelation is a resource for everyone, but readers must not get caught up in what cannot be fully understood or may cause fear. Over time, with focused study, greater understanding will come. Christians know that greater biblical knowledge and understanding will continue to increase until Jesus returns, but they must patiently wait on Him. The devil and the world delight in fear and intimidation, but these are no match for God, His angels, or Christ's light shining through Christians who love God's Word.

Christians must be strong and keep their heads out of the sand. Spiritual warfare is real. No one can know when Jesus will return, but Christians can be prepared. We do know, almost instantaneously, what is happening all over the world, so when Jesus does come the news will travel fast. When people deliberately sin against God's laws, they occupy a position of lawlessness, which is characteristic of life close to Jesus's return. Lawlessness is lovelessness. Laodicea had no love or truth; it was self-sufficient and worldly, apt descriptors of our world today.

The Seven Blessings of Revelation

Revelation is a blessing for all who read, study, share, discuss, and pray about it. The seven blessings of Revelation begin with "Blessed is" or "Blessed are."

1. *Blessed for Reading and Heeding God's Word*

> Blessed is the one who reads aloud the words of this prophecy, and blessed are those who hear, and who keep what is written in it, for the time is near. (Rev. 1:3)[104]

There is nothing quite like reading the Bible aloud or listening to it being read and following along in it. It is balm for a weary body. In difficult times, the Bible is good medicine for an aching heart. It is tonic for a troubled soul, refreshing every cell of the body. Knowing that you are blessed is life-giving. Knowing that in the power of the Holy Spirit you are honestly and humbly doing your best to be in

---

[104] See Luke 11:28. Jesus's reply to a woman who says to Him, "Blessed is the womb that bore you, and the breasts at which you nursed!" is *"Blessed rather are those who hear the word of God and keep it!"*

God's will, keeping His commandments and laws and repenting after sin, and receiving God's forgiveness every time you fall is to be doubly blessed.

2. *Blessed Are the Dead in the Lord*

> And I heard a voice from heaven saying, "Write this: Blessed are the dead who die in the Lord from now on." "Blessed indeed," says the Spirit, "that they may rest from their labors, for their deeds follow them!" (Rev. 14:13)

Christians are reassured to know that their loved ones who endured in the Lord, keeping the commandments and faith in Jesus, are blessed with rest from their labors upon death. This blessing arrives just before the first harvest of the earth, when Jesus gathers wheat or barley (Rev. 14:14–16), beginning with the martyrs, the firstfruits in verse 4. Afterwards, angels gather grapes from the vine of the earth in the second harvest (Rev. 14:17–20) to be placed in the "great winepress of the wrath of God," which causes great consternation to some.

Christians trust God to know them, and they trust the Bible. They do not believe that everyone passes into eternal life and receives angel wings along the way. The Bible clearly states that humans are created lower than angels and that when they die, they are judged by Jesus. Christians know, that when they die and are judged by Jesus, they become higher than angels, and judge them (Ps. 8:5; Heb. 2:7; 1 Cor. 6:3).

3. *Blessed Are the Prepared*

> (Behold, I am coming like a thief! Blessed is the one who stays awake, keeping his garments on, that he may not go about naked and be seen exposed!) (Rev. 16:15)

Christians throughout history knew the importance of being spiritually vigilant and ready for the day when Jesus would return. They are dressed and prepared. Non-Christians either are oblivious to Jesus or against Him. They are naked and exposed. All who live a redeemed life are blessed and will not be caught off guard when Jesus comes to earth again. Praying for the salvation of their loved ones, they entrust them lovingly to God's care and provision.

4. *Blessed Is the Bride of Christ*

> And the angel said to me, "Write this: Blessed are those who are invited to the marriage supper of the Lamb." And he said to me, "These are the true words of God." (Rev. 19:9)

The marriage supper of the Lamb exceeds every special world event. What a privilege to be present for this wedding feast. The invited are worthy, having kept the Word of God to the end. The church, the Bride of Christ, is radiant, washed pure, and clothed with the righteousness of Christ. All Christians will be blessed by the celebration of Jesus's uniting with His body, the church.

5. *Blessed Are the First Resurrected*

> Blessed and holy is the one who shares in the first resurrection! Over such the second death has no power, but they will be priests of God and of Christ, and they will reign with him for a thousand years. (Rev. 20:6)

Christians share in Christ's resurrection. There is no second death for those saved and purified by Jesus's blood. They will be heirs with Christ and priests of God. This last verse of a description of a millennial period (Rev. 20:1–6) suggests two resurrections. Those "beheaded for the testimony of Jesus and the Word of God, and those who had not worshipped the beast or its image and had not received its mark on their foreheads or their hands" may be interpreted as those who will be martyred during the tribulation. These will reign with Christ in what some term the Martyrs' Reign (Rev. 20:4–5).[105] Much about faith is miraculous and mysterious. Christians do not know, and they cannot understand the entire Bible, but they do believe and trust in Jesus, knowing that all things will work together for the good of those who know and love Him. How this will happen no one knows. Belief in God is what the Bible says matters.

6. *Blessed Are Those Who Keep the Words of Prophecy*

> And behold, I am coming soon. Blessed is the one who keeps the words of the prophecy of this book. (Rev. 22:7)

Jesus is coming soon. What a blessed assurance for Christians who care about the eternal security of those they love. Only Jesus will judge—Christians trust Him to love perfectly and to judge justly and fairly. Keeping the words of the prophecy of Revelation means that Christians must read them, digest them, and pray for understanding and wisdom about them so that they themselves may be preserved. The veracity of God's Word is emphasized seven times in the last two chapters of Revelation: in 21:5, and 22:6, 7, 9, 10, and the solemn warnings in 22:18, 19. Every word from the beginning of Genesis to the last verse of Revelation is holy.

7. *Blessed Are the Repentant*

> Blessed are those who wash their robes, so that they may have the right to the tree of life and that they may enter the city by the gates. (Rev. 22:14)

---

[105] This is one of the most controversial sections in Revelation. Three main views are 1) premillennialism, those believing Christ will return before the millennium of peace and justice before Satan is defeated and all are judged, 2) postmillennialism, those believing Christ will return after the millennium, and 3) amillennialism, those holding a non-literal millennial view, believing the thousand years is the present church age we live in, and there is no future millennium before Christ returns for the final judgment.

The faithful repent as soon as they sin because they know that they have sinned against God and that they will be forgiven. Never again will they be outside of God's will by loving lies, evil, and murder. Not only do they have the right to the tree of life but they will also enter heaven. All the repentant will live eternally with Jesus.

Heaven displays God's love and blessings as He intends, not as the world thinks or determines. It is filled with God's great goodness and full justice. Non-Christians do not understand what it will mean to be in heaven—it will not be what they dream of or even want. Those resistant to God's will on earth will not know heaven unless they repent. Heaven is God's place, but it is prepared for all who love Him. Christians long for it because they love God and what He loves. A person must first repent and believe in Jesus before he or she can enter heaven. Growing closer to God, loving what He loves, and hating what He hates will prepare them for heaven and for all of eternity.

Encouragement from Antiquity—Who Is This Jesus?

Only two of the seven churches were awake and ready for judgment and heaven, but the faithful from the five other churches knew Scripture and held their churches accountable to it. Their work continues to bless the church today. Christians who work diligently to spread the gospel are part of the remnant that God ensures will be present in every generation until Jesus ushers in a new heaven and a new earth. Until then, Christians keep the faith, knowing that Christ is victorious on earth and in heaven, even as the battle for souls rages around them.

The church in Sardis was spiritually deficient in the first century, but some Christians there, such as Bishop Melito in the second century, were faithful. We do not know how many were faithful, nor for how long this church remained faithful. The witness of Melito was preserved by Polycrates of Ephesus, Hippolytus, and Tertullian. Many of Melito's works, now lost, were cited by Eusebius. Melito did not agree with all the positions taken by the Roman church, but he was greatly respected. His succinct treatise on the divinity of Christ has been translated by Dr. James White:

Who Is This Jesus?

And so he was lifted upon a tree and an inscription was attached indicating who was being killed. Who was it? It is a grievous thing to tell, but a most fearful thing to refrain from telling. But listen, as you tremble before him on whose account the earth trembled!

He who hung the earth in place is hanged.

He who fixed the heavens in place is fixed in place.

He who made all things fast is made fast on a tree.

The Sovereign is insulted.

God is murdered.

The King of Israel is destroyed by an Israelite hand.

This is the One who made the heavens and the earth,

and formed mankind in the beginning,

The One proclaimed by the Law and the Prophets,

The One enfleshed in a virgin,

The One hanged on a tree.

The One buried in the earth,

The One raised from the dead and who went up into the heights of heaven,

The One sitting at the right hand of the Father,

The One having all authority to judge and save,

Through Whom the Father made the things which exist from the beginning of time.

This One is "the Alpha and the Omega,"

This One is "the beginning and the end"

The beginning indescribable and the end incomprehensible.

This One is the Christ.

This One is the King.

This One is Jesus.

This One is the Leader.

This One is the Lord.

This One is the One who rose from the dead.

This One is the One sitting on the right hand of the Father.

He bears the Father and is borne by the Father.

"To him be the glory and the power forever. Amen."[106]

Until Jesus Returns

The Triune God is the same yesterday, today, and tomorrow. What Jesus revealed to the church in John's day applies today. The church must study and understand Jesus's messages. According to the Bible, in the last days people will refuse to listen (2 Tim. 4:4). They will continue sinning, which is not what God desires.[107] These words have been true from the time of Jesus—the beginning of the last days. God will not force Himself on anyone. The faithful follow the Bible because they want to be faithful to God first, like Smyrna and Philadelphia were.

Sometimes biblical truth is accidentally or deliberately omitted, covered up, or watered down by religious institutions, as the five lost Revelation churches may have done. This greatly displeases but does not surprise God. His Word is clear on what is necessary to faith. Salvation comes through Jesus, not through a pastor, priest, angel, or good works, but if people know Jesus, they work to serve Him out of love. Ultimately, "faith without works is dead" (James 2:17). Christians are one in spirit and truth, knowing that if they reject God, He will reject them (Hos. 4:6).

The Bible is clear. Without God's Word, and the discipline to

---

[106] "Who Is This Jesus? By Melito of Sardis," posted by John Samson, February 25, 2006; accessed January 7, 2020, www.reformationtheology.com/2006/02/who_is_this_jesus_by_melito_of.php. This is part of Melito's sermon on the Passover which he preached about 180 AD, over a hundred years before Constantine's battle on the Milvian Bridge in 312 AD and the First Council of Nicaea in 325 AD.
[107] See Ezek. 18:23; Rom. 1:24; Heb. 6:4–6.

study and teach it appropriately, the church will perish.[108] Christians consistently preach and teach the truth in love (Eph. 4:15), even in areas hostile to the Bible, despite threats on their lives. Many biblical concepts are difficult, especially for non-Christians. Even the apostles found Jesus's teachings difficult at first (John 6:60–66). After His teaching "I am the bread of life," some questioned His identity and grumbled among themselves. God rewards those who persist in Bible reading and study. It teaches the right way to live, but unbelief results in spiritual death. In the scope of eternity, a lifetime, no matter its length, is extremely brief. Jesus meets people where they are so that they may know God through Him. He makes the binary clear: "Whoever is not with me is against me," (Matt. 12:30a).[109] Those following Christ are of and for Him.

God works through people to accomplish His will and bring family, friends, strangers, and even enemies to Himself. Jesus and the Holy Spirit also work in and through people, in visions, in the pain of everyday life, and through the Bible. Bible study brings people into relationship with each other and with God. God's Word influenced the world for thousands of years. Many do not read it; some hate it. Some who hold to worldly, human traditions, as a means of salvation, are oblivious to it. "You leave the commandment of God and hold to the tradition of men," said Jesus, in verse 8 of a section on traditions and commandments (Mark 7:1–13). The Pharisees and the scribes asked Jesus why His followers did not adhere to the tradition of the elders but ate with defiled hands. Jesus rebuked them; He knew what they were trying to do: "Well did Isaiah prophecy of you hypocrites, as it is written, 'This people honors me with their lips, but their heart is far from me; in vain do they worship me, teaching as doctrines the commandments of men.'" Their manmade traditions had become more important than the Word of God. Those following Jesus, however, had not broken Mosaic law but later manmade Jewish traditions: the ritual washing of hands, utensils, and furniture. Jesus taught that human traditions were optional but God's laws

---

[108] See Job 36:12; Prov. 5:23; 10:21; 29:18.
[109] See also Mark 9:40; Luke 11:23.

could not be disobeyed or ignored. It is more important to obey God's commandments and worship Him than to wash one's hands.[110]

From its beginning, the church studied God's words, as Israel had. Faithful leaders study them so that they can teach and live by them, as Jesus did. God calls His people to be obedient, but obedience is not highly regarded today. Jesus told the seven churches to teach truth in love—including discipline and obedience—out of love for God and not to fulfill fleshly desires or bend to a fickle, ever-changing, dying world. Churches are responsible for their leaders—the first whom Jesus will hold accountable on judgment day. Revelation's letters are clear: all sin must be addressed.

Believing parents, grandparents, and teachers give children whom they love what they need, not what they want, as God does for us. They do not equate loving a child, parent, or anyone else with loving their sin. Sin is detestable in God's eyes, and it will be dealt with by a holy God. By being obedient, Jesus took our sins away, providing an open door to eternity. Knowing the Bible helps Christians understand what is necessary for salvation and how to patiently endure and be awake and ready for the end.

> Therefore, stay awake, for you do not know on what day your Lord is coming. But know this, that if the master of the house had known in what part of the night the thief was coming, he would have stayed awake and would not have let his house be broken into. Therefore you also must be ready, for the Son of Man is coming at an hour you do not expect. (Matt. 24:42–44)

God bears up the faithful to bring as many into the kingdom as He has determined before Jesus returns. A remnant of alert, bold

---

[110] Knowing the origin of hand washing is interesting but Jesus's message pertains to more than the washing of hands. It is about where we place God in our lives. Most people have no idea as to where regular hand washing began. It originated in the Hebrew Scripture, as did other health practices that continued into the Old and New Testaments (e.g., Lev. 15:1–16; Isa. 1:16–20; Mark 7:1–23). So much is lost through Bible ignorance.

Christians around the world serve Him in love, honesty, and truth because they follow Jesus and the Bible. The church knows the mighty God it serves, but unrepentant sinners within church bodies do not. Life is breathed into every Christian by the Holy Spirit. The letters of Jesus's revelation provide nourishment for this life and hope of the future eternal one with Him, as Christians pray for strength to bear up until death or until Christ returns.

Our days are rife with abuse, confusion, deception, denial, and perversion, and that, according to the Bible, will only increase.[111] Christians thank God that He has provided the way to persevere and survive through the sacrifice of Jesus, by God's Word, and in the Holy Spirit. Jesus tells us in the seven letters what will save souls.

Through Jesus, the remnant has direct access to God. It always leans on God, His Word, Jesus, and the power of the Holy Spirit, especially in troublesome times. The remnant knows that God's redemption for its sin was costly. Christians' lives also come at a price and are for a purpose. The enemy seeks to destroy, distract, and defile as many as he can by sowing unbelief, selfishness, and/or pride. God is worshipped and praised for who He is, not because of what He has done, can, or will do. He is worthy of honor, praise, and glory because He is God. Christians want to change as God wants them to change so that they are closer to Him, and less like the world that is totally out of control.

Near the end of Revelation, Jesus, accompanied by the resurrected saints of the church, returns to claim His bride in Jerusalem. Some believe that the bride will be a Jewish remnant which follows Jesus as Messiah. Others believe it is the church,

---

[111] People choose now what years ago were off limits: gender, time to live, and time to die. At least one church leader was as disenfranchised by the church she served as by the world. Living as a transgender woman, Abby was elated to be accepted into Christian ministry but troubled by a directive from her governing board. She was told that, to serve her church, she must refrain from naming *Jesus,* as this was too exclusive. While changing gender was irrelevant to both her and the board, Abby was troubled by the directive that banned her from saying Jesus's name. It caused her to question how she could show faith in Jesus and not name Him. As seen in this example, confusion, even in what is "the church," is rampant. The name in this personal anecdote is changed to protect the identity of the individual.

both Jewish and Gentile Christians. Presently Jerusalem is divided into Armenian, Christian, Jewish, and Muslim quarters around what was the Second Temple, the temple that Jesus attended. Some believe that a third temple must be built before His return. Prophetic dates and end-time topics such as the rapture, millennialism, and tribulation deriving from Revelation, Matthew, 1 and 2 Thessalonians, Daniel, and Zechariah are captivating, but prophecy is not the remnant's focus. Staying true to God and His Word through Christ and witnessing for Him in His love as long as they live, is.

Jerusalem with the Temple Mount in the center.

Immediately following the seven letters, in Revelation 4:1, from the open door in heaven's throne room, Jesus spoke to John with a voice like a trumpet: "Come up here, and I will show you what must take place after this." Again, Jesus uses the command "to come." John obeys and witnesses God and His rainbow encased throne (Rev. 4:2–3). Whether what follows describes a pre-tribulation rapture is not what is most important. Trusting God and His Word to live within God's will is.

Faith in Jesus gets people through the harrowing times in their lives. It provides a means of coping with the animosity and uncertainty of an increasingly chaotic world as believing minds are opened to the futility of faith in humankind. They do not worry about the details of what will happen before Jesus returns for the second time. They know that Jesus will return because God's revelation through John for the world tells them He will.

Everything in Revelation is reliable and trustworthy but much of it will only be understood as it unfolds. The remnant patiently and faithfully endures all that comes, joyfully anticipating and lovingly upholding and teaching God's truth to reach as many as possible with the gospel before this happens. Christians do this because they are loved with the greatest love that there is.

Maranatha.[112] Come, Lord Jesus, come.

Lydia of Thyatira was baptized in this stream in Philippi.

---

[112] Matthew Easton, "Maranatha," accessed September 23, 2020, https://www.biblestudytools.com/dictionary/maranatha/. *Maranatha*, composed of two Armenian words, means that Jesus is coming, and He will judge. It is only found once in the Bible (1 Cor. 16:22).

Loved beyond Measure

> Do you not know that your bodies are temples of the
> Holy Spirit, who is in you, whom you have received
> from God? You are not your own; you were bought
> at a price. Therefore honor God with your bodies. (1
> Cor. 6:19–20 NIV)

Jesus's death was a result of the greatest love there is. His selfless act enables all to choose to be temples of the Holy Spirit and to live eternally with God. Every Christian of Revelation's seven churches felt God's love and knew its great cost. Every person must decide to accept the greatest love there is.

Some people need to be convinced that Jesus is who He says He is. The apostle Paul was such a person. His Damascus Road conversion was dramatic, maybe because God had a monumental plan for his life. The conversion and baptism of Lydia of Thyatira, in Philippi, where Paul founded Europe's first church, greatly changed her life, but these events were not spectacular. A wealthy seller of purple, who needed nothing, this woman found something in Christ that she could not live without. Believing in and following Jesus as Lord is about being perfectly known and loved for who you are, while at the same time being made whole and worthy of God's love, as Paul and Lydia were.

John knew Jesus's love firsthand. He passed that love on to everyone he encountered, but he likely did not fully understand everything that Jesus told him to write in Revelation. We too know that fully understanding this book is impossible, but we can take what we know for sure, such as the letters to the seven churches, and use it for God. Nothing is withheld that Jesus wants revealed, and everything will come to fruition in His time, as Christians are enabled to do all things through the Holy Spirit who strengthens them. Jesus's challenge for them is to live out God's truth with His love as John, Paul, and Lydia did, and as all Christians do. Christians know that only God does the saving, but as temples of the Holy Spirit, they can direct others to the vine, to Jesus.

Revelation encapsulates everything, explicitly or implicitly, from creation to Jesus's return and establishment of the new heaven and the new earth, because it is of Him. Jesus's message progresses step by step, just as knowledge of who God is progressively increases in the Bible. We only understand what we do at any given time because God knows our limits. Reading Revelation is like peeling an onion. We do not know the number of layers beneath the surface, what will be found, or the tears that will be shed. But we do know that God's love for us is immeasurable and that He is ever-present with us.

Loved and Grateful

Nothing is more precious than God's love for us. We may love many, and be loved by many, but every person is flawed and eventually dies. God's love is eternally perfect. When His love is rejected, heartache, pain, and suffering ensue. Ephesus found out what it meant to spurn God's love. It died, and its inhabitants were lost forever.

Most churches teach the importance of love, but far too often it is a sentimental, shallow love, not God's deep agape love. Unless we experience God's love ourselves, we have no hope of describing it to others. Even then, God's perfect love often defies description. Transformed people, though, help others see this love.

God's love reciprocated indicates when a person is redeemed, as Christians relate to others as God loves them. This does not mean that Christians are weak and easily duped. Under the transformative power of the Holy Spirit, they wisely live as God directs. They mirror God's measureless love that comes to them. Those who are happy with their pagan lifestyles cannot relate to the one true God, despite His love for them. They cannot see through their sin. Those united with God's Spirit relate spiritually with Him and therefore relate differently to others, as they live beyond a purely physical realm into God's spiritual realm.

Worldly love cannot be compared to God's love. Regardless of emotions and feelings, everything good, right, and true stems from

God. Only God's love is immortal. Worldly love—phileo, eros, and storge—lasts for a season. The most skilled, esteemed physicians have patients who die. They too one day will die. The ability to heal and love comes from God but means little if souls are lost. Our agape love for God means accepting Jesus and His sacrificial atonement so that we are in right relationship with God. This causes difficulty for those who would like to believe that God can be accessed in any way. Everyone must weigh the evidence of the cross of Christ for themselves, come to terms with it, and choose whom to follow.

With right beliefs, people are brought into direct relationship with God, not with Christian friends or families, nor with the church, although other Christians and the church may assist non-Christians in taking their first step. It is God's work on people's hearts that makes them into temples of the Holy Spirit so that they may glorify God in their lives, treasure their bodies, and promote Christ's love and truth. Christians love God as Father and are members of His household. Those knowing God's love are extremely grateful for life, for God's call, and for the freedom to worship Him. They thank God for His transforming them into His children, for providing godly perception, and for the ability to love and pray for others. Seeds of faith sown during their lives continue to live and work on the hearts and minds of those prayed for long after they have died.[113]

Expressing gratitude to God comes naturally to Christians, because they are thankful for all that Jesus has done and is doing in their lives. They give thanks for those who have impacted their lives with the love of God and the truth of the gospel.[114] Loving God

---

[113] Examples include the apostles, the martyrs of the Bible, Melito of Sardis, the author of "The Fellowship of the Unashamed," John Bunyan, countless Christian authors, innumerable martyrs of the church, and deceased family members and friends.

[114] One personal and moving example is the record of the native American *Squanto* (or *Tisquantum*) who was abducted and sold into slavery. Squanto's life is indicative of the evil of the seventeenth century but even more indicative of God's love and grace. Helped by monks in Spain, Squanto was sent to England, where he stayed with a merchant before boarding a ship crossing the Atlantic which stopped at Cupids, Newfoundland, before returning to Massachusetts. Squanto's Newfoundland stay contributed to what is considered the first Thanksgiving. The

first before anything else causes Christians to want to obey God and live as He wants them to live. They want to be His beloved because they understand how sin involves idolatry and separates them from God. Idolatry must be repented of. Loving God helps them to want to keep His commands and laws, especially the ninth commandment, and genuinely love others as God does. Truth builds Christians in the right direction, toward God. Anything less than complete honesty is in the opposite direction, is corrupt, and is of another spirit.

> Praise the LORD!
> Oh give thanks to the LORD, for he is good,
> for his steadfast love endures forever! (Ps. 106:1)

Love in Tension with Sin

"If it feels good do it" seems to be as true for Christians as for non-Christians. What we read, see, or hear on television or social media leads us to believe that life is all about looking good, feeling pleasure, and being happy. Too many people profess God yet live like the world lives. The rational mind is easily tricked into doubting faith, especially when life is abundant and pleasurable. This is especially true when the culture teaches that truth depends on individuals' personal truth.

The letters that John sent the seven churches speak wisdom to Christians in the twenty-first century as they did in the first century. Ephesus teaches that loving God and His truth must come first. Christians learn about evil and the devil from Pergamum. Thyatira teaches the importance of controlling the sinful desires of our physical bodies, as sin makes its home in many who think they are good, kind people, according to Sardis. They learn how easy it is to be totally deluded and eternally lost from Laodicea. Smyrna and Philadelphia teach that it is possible to be faithful and hold God's truth in tandem

---

author lives about fifty-five miles from Cupids, whose museum has a picture of Squanto. A children's version of his life, written by Eric Metaxas, *Squanto and the Miracle of Thanksgiving* (Nashville, TN: Tommy Nelson, 2012), mentions Newfoundland.

with His love. All seven churches teach the hope of repentance through Christ. Every time they fall, they repent, try harder, and pray more. They pray for loved ones and for "forward-thinking" churches who profess faith but believe that the Bible is obsolete.

Putting God first and living God's way in hope of eternal life with Him is not only unpopular today but it is ridiculed by all who believe that everyone's truth is of equal value. A strong work ethic is generally expected, but few know that the source of such a work ethic is biblical. In many cases work itself is idolized. God warns us not to worship anything but Him, which means that we must battle our flesh, the world, and the devil, and we must go through Jesus to reach God.[115] Constant Bible study equips Christians with wisdom and discernment to fight error when they sin, or are exposed to something harmful, such as questionable "Christian" literature. Christians know that everyone will be judged at the great white throne in heaven (Rev. 20:13).[116] Non-Christians will be condemned for their sins, while Christians, named in the book of life, will enter the new heaven and the new earth, with their deeds determining their rewards (Matt. 16:27).

Being true to God is impossible for those "Christians" who resemble the non-Christians of the five faithless churches of Revelation, according to Jesus. Without the indwelling Holy Spirit, biblical wisdom, and prayer, "Christians" who do what looks good and feels pleasurable are lost. Beauty appeals mainly to feelings, and it causes tension between soul and spirit and between our flesh and God. No one pleases God by living in opposition to what He says is right. By submitting to temptation, our bodies are not honored as God says they should be. Nothing of Jesus's appearance is known, yet we know that the devil was thrown from heaven due to his pride in his own appearance.

---

[115] See John 14:6; Acts 4:12; 1 Tim. 2:5.

[116] "The nations raged, but your wrath came, and the time for the dead to be judged, and for rewarding your servants, the prophets and saints, and those who fear your name, both small and great, and for destroying the destroyers of the earth" (Rev. 11:18). See also 1 Thess. 4:13–18.

The devil creates tension between Christians and God while he has permission to rule the world. He tempts everyone to turn away from God and worship him instead. Tension builds between Christians and those who think that they are Christians but who straddle God's ways and the world as Pergamum, Thyatira, Sardis, and Laodicea did. Comfortable faith like that of Sardis and Laodicea is harder to fight than a pagan faith like that of Ephesus, because the Bible is just one of many "holy" books. Satan waits to lure who he can, but his darkness masquerading as light is no match for Christ's light.

The Bible is light, as God is light. It lightens a narrow path in a dark, ugly world. It is hated just as God's ways and His people are hated, but it is the perfect litmus test of faithfulness. The Bible's ultimate truth inspires the righteous to be wary and wise as they, armed by the Spirit, carefully tread the fine winding path to battle the devil's evil.

A favorite country and western song requested in Christian prison programs, "Choices" by Billy Yates and Mike Curtis, sung by George Jones, is about those choices in life that lead down a broad road, not the narrow path of Jesus. "I've had choices / Since the day that I was born / There were voices / That told me right from wrong / If I had listened / No, I wouldn't be here today / Living and dying / With the choices I made / ..." Many things on that broad road are against God and for our own deluded sense of pleasure, the devil, and the world. Men and women worldwide find and experience God's love in prison. They understand that there is no greater love or freedom than that found in Jesus. If they choose Him, they are free indeed.[117] Everyone can choose this absolute freedom in Christ.

> For we must all appear before the judgment seat of Christ, so that each one may receive what is due for what he has done in the body, whether good or evil. (2 Cor. 5:10; see also Matt. 16:27 and Rom. 14:10)

---

[117] At least one Bible used in prisons emphasizes freedom: The Canadian Bible Society's *The Key to Freedom*. See n. 33.

The Bema Seat in Corinth's marketplace, where
Paul was brought before the tribunal.

> Your words were found, and I ate them, and your words became to me a joy and the delight of my heart, for I am called by your name, O Lord God of hosts. (Jer. 15:16)

Jeremiah withstood persistent persecution because of God's love. Despite preaching the truth in love, Jeremiah only ever converted Baruck, his secretary, and Ebed-melech, an Ethiopian eunuch. But, Jeremiah left a phenomenal spiritual heritage. His own words are part of the Word of God that he delighted in. We too must delight in God's Word as Jeremiah did.

Christians know that God is great, and good—according to His definitions, not theirs. God can do anything, even remove all Christians from the earth before life becomes unbearable, but no one knows for sure if He will. Christians patiently endure. Living in an age when the Bible is available to most, but where many do not appreciate or use it wisely, twenty-first-century Christians read, live, and teach it. With the world vehemently anti-Christ, Jesus is more needed and better news than ever before.

First-century Christians found encouragement and strength in their pain-filled world in the Psalms and Proverbs, as we do today. Solomon, who wrote many of the Proverbs, asked God for wisdom, and God granted his request. God also gave him wealth, but Solomon dealt poorly with it and the many foreign women whom he married. The Proverbs, rich reminders of God's ways, help Christians value and stay true to their priceless salvation. Proverbs 3:5–7 is the basis of the song "Trust": "Trust in the Lord with all your heart, / and do not lean on your own understanding. / In all your ways acknowledge him, / and he will make straight your paths. / Be not wise in your own eyes; / fear the Lord and turn away from evil."[118]

The Psalms point Christians to God's truth. David, author of many of the psalms, loved to sing and play them on his harp. The

---

[118] "Trust," accessed August 3, 2020, https://www.youtube.com/watch?v=oCLK9P7kh6Y.

internet is a vast source of inspirational Christian music to buoy us up. One hymn, based on Psalm 5:8, "Lead Me Lord," written by Samuel Wesley, grandson of Charles Wesley, is a deep, heartfelt prayer that people can use to request God's clear and righteous guidance along life's narrow path of Christian faith.[119]

Whose we are and what we learn while we live in these bodies of flesh is the same today as it was in the first century. Faith is determined by whom we follow and what we allow ourselves to learn. If we are not morally and spiritually astute, we can lose our souls as easily as five of the seven churches did. In Christ, we are led to dependence upon God, to totally trust Him and allow Him to love us with that joyous love that defies all description. If we trust in ourselves, we are lost.

As in the first century, life is difficult for most. Some are unwanted at birth, or may never have bonded with, or know, their parents. Others are born with or later develop serious illnesses, while others deal with what seems like inferior and/or more difficult lives than most. Many like the darkness outside of God's will. God wants everyone to know that they are not mistakes. As our creator, He knew us before we were formed in our mothers' wombs. God does not take revenge on people. What may look like His revenge is often the consequences of people's wrong choices and/or the actions of the devil. God's will, God's way, and God's Word are perfect. As imperfect, created beings, people are wisest when they "live their best lives" through relinquishing their own stubborn wills and allow the Holy Spirit to direct them to God.

Christians submit themselves to God's will, which means He can guide them into a wholesome life in preparation for the next. They purposefully choose God's perfect will over their flawed will and allow God to rule their lives. Christians cannot walk the earth physically with Jesus, but His indwelling Holy Spirit comforts, guides, and directs them away from sins of the flesh, the world, and the devil. The Bible is the firm foundation for knowing. Prayer is an essential

[119] "Lead Me Lord (in Your Righteousness)," accessed August 3, 2020, https://www.youtube.com/watch?v=XLtlyIXJ3V4.

part of every Christian's breath. Jesus prayed much and gave His church the perfect prayer: the "Lord's Prayer" (Matt. 6:9–13), also known as the "Our Father" (Appendix II). This is the only prayer Jesus directed His followers to use to help them draw closer to God.

For Christians, every day is more fulfilling than the last, as each day's walk with God helps them to let go more of what the world wants and leads them to what they need. Each new day allows them to accept more of God's goodness and what He knows is best for them. As they are tried and tested, they hold on to all that is holy, right, and true because of God's love. Progressive sanctification helps them to be more faithful to God, with fewer doubts, until eventually they are fearless through Christ who saves them and through the indwelling Holy Spirit who carries them. Every day they become bolder witnesses for Jesus. They are courageous like the churches of Smyrna and Philadelphia and do not fear anything of the world—people, power, or science—but they do not worship them either. Christians are free to explore and discover the beauty of God's world, including His laws. God wants us to love all that is good and beautiful in His creation. Through faith, we learn to trust God in every moment, especially during pain, suffering, and heartache. People disappoint us and they lie, steal, cheat, leave, and die, but God is ever-present. With His help, we are emboldened to speak His absolute truth in love to those we love, and whom God places purposefully in our path. And we love them as God loves them.

The church has always been sifted and shaken, but increasing confusion over what Christians believe in recent decades has caused more to avoid it. Christians know that there is sin in the church but many refuse to speak out. God desires that the faithful stand for Him, but many prefer to leave churches rather than fight what is ungodly inside of them. One day both those inside and outside the church will be held accountable.

Jesus's birth impacted the world like nothing else ever has. Eusebius documented the great darkness and unrest of the first three centuries. His writings support the Bible and the early church fathers. Although corruption infiltrates churches, and individuals sin greatly, we can learn from and be deeply encouraged by strong and loving Christians. The faithful body of Christians must learn from and grow past the hurt done falsely in the name of Christ; much greater good than wrong has been done in Jesus's name. Godly love, which God has for us and which He expects us to have for others, was the love exemplified by John, the other apostles, and the faithful early church—all willing to give their lives so that others might hear the truth of the gospel. We too, in our day, must love God enough to be willing to die for Him.

Jesus's revelation tells us what we must know to follow the straight and narrow path of living, loving, and heaven. The letters to the seven churches summarize how to inherit eternal life: God must be loved through Jesus and God's ways must be followed. Being within God's will changes people to be His instruments of hope and love in an evil world that hates Him and is decaying before our eyes. Some have never heard Jesus's letters to the seven churches or of the book of Revelation. Many died before it was written. Others never had the opportunity to hear or read it themselves. Many were unable to read it. Some places—Laodicea may have been just such a place—purposely withheld Jesus's revelation. But Revelation is available to much of the world today.

Bible study and prayer change people when they are receptive to it. How easily people's hearts turn toward God through the truth that He reveals. Lydia of Thyatira was saved long before the writing of Revelation. She may not have heard or read it, but she found the greatest love of all, and knew Jesus through Paul, the Old Testament, and the early New Testament writings. Lydia may have heard of her conversion immortalized in Acts 16. This woman, whom some place on an apostolic level, exemplifies a person who makes the best choice anyone can make—choosing Jesus and eternity.

We do not know how many have heard or read Revelation or how many lives have been changed by it. Melito of Sardis probably was impacted by Revelation because he wrote about it. With the world as confused and wicked as it is, offering so little hope, there is a great need to read the Bible and understand the hope of Jesus and the power of God. The letters to the seven churches explain well who Jesus is and what God expects of anyone who wants to know Him and live eternally with Him.

The question for non-Christians is, "Do you want to know the greatest love there is?" If so, Revelation is an appropriate place to start. According to it, heaven and hell are real. Judgment is real. But these are not daunting when people know God through Christ. There is no fear, only faith in a much bigger, greater tomorrow, whatever it entails. Faith, hope, and love. The greatest is love. No greater love exists than God's love. It is the beginning of all love, faith, hope, true joy, and everlasting peace. Through Revelation, Jesus invites everyone to experience God's love for themselves. It is the greatest love in and for all the people in the world.

> Rejoice in the Lord always; again I will say, Rejoice. Let your reasonableness be known to everyone. The Lord is at hand; do not be anxious about anything, but in everything by prayer and supplication with thanksgiving let your requests be made known to God. And the peace of God, which surpasses all understanding, will guard your hearts and your minds in Christ Jesus. Finally, brothers, whatever is true, whatever is honorable, whatever is just, whatever is pure, whatever is lovely, whatever is commendable, if there is any excellence, if there is anything worthy of praise, think about these things. (Phil. 4:4–8).

Interior, Greek Orthodox Church dedicated to the Equal-
to-the-Apostles Lydia of Thyatira, Krynides, Greece.

APPENDICES

APPENDICES

APPENDIX 1

Christian Paradigms

#	Time Period	Contributing Factors	Paradigm	Also Note
1	c.3 BC to 28–33 AD	Jesus's life: miracles, teachings, crucifixion, resurrection, ascension.	*Jesus*	John the Baptist, Second Temple, Hebrew Scripture.
2	33–100 AD Pentecost, to John's death	From Jerusalem to Judea, Samaria, Asia, Crimea, Egypt, India, & Rome, early heresy, early persecution.	*Apostolic Age Inception and Institution of the Church*	Apostles and 500 disciples build the church, Stephen is the first martyr, Christian Scriptures.
3	101–312 AD End of Apostolic Age to Battle at Milvian Bridge	3 centers: Alexandria, Antioch, & Rome, Biblical canon, more heresy, church goes underground due to greater persecution.	*Early/ Great Church*	Church fathers: Ignatius of Antioch, Clement of Alexandria, Polycarp, Irenaeus, Melito of Sardis, Origen, Tertullian, Justin Martyr, etc.
4	313–475 AD Western Roman Empire collapse	Emperor Constantine, Constantinople feuds, much greater heresy, Arianism vs. Orthodoxy.	*Acceptance of Christianity*	Eusebius, Augustine, Theodosius I & the state church (380), monasticism begins.
5	476–799 AD	5 centers: Jerusalem & Constantinople added, errors and schisms.	*Early Middle Ages*	Justinian I initiates the Pentarchy, disputes over icons.
6	800–1299 AD	Crusades, corruption, medieval inquisition.	*Middle Ages*	Anselm, the Great Schism of 1054.
7	1300–1499 AD	Corruption increases, western schism ends.	*Late Middle Ages*	Wycliffe, Huss, Constantinople falls.
8	1500–1684 AD	Orthodoxy, the Bible, Galileo's trial (1633), Missions, philosophy, Puritans (N. America).	*Early Modern Age Reformation*	Tyndale, Erasmus, Luther, Zwingli, Calvin, Pascal, Descartes, piety.
9	1685–1815 AD	Enlightenment (Kant), scientific racism.	*Age of Reason*	Great Awakenings, John Wesley.
10	1816–1899 AD	Democracy, socialism, end of slavery (1865), liberal theology.	*Late Modern Age Human Might*	Science, evolution, hierarchy of man, colonialism, nihilism.
11	1900–1999	Pentecostalism, world wars, Holocaust, sexual revolution, liberation theology.	*Postmodern Liberalism*	Dead Sea Scrolls, WCC (1948), Roe vs. Wade (1973), church scandals surface.
12	2000–present	Power, lies, deceit, individualism, racism, environmentalism, politics, extremism.	*Anti-Bible, Anti-God, and Anti-Christian*	Left–Right, lobbies, social justice/protest, progressivism, worldwide viruses.

The first paradigm covers the first third of the first century. It follows the life of Jesus in the Second Temple period running from before His birth through His ministry, miracles, death, resurrection, and ascension. John the Baptist led the way. The second paradigm begins at Pentecost with the coming of the Holy Spirit. It marks the beginning of the church, which includes persecution, sacrifice, and heresy. It ends with the death of the last apostle, John (c.100 AD). New Testament writings are added to the Hebrew Scripture that Jesus used in His teachings.

After the apostle John's death, the third paradigm begins. The expansion of the early church runs until the battle at the Milvian Bridge/Constantine's conversion (c.312 AD). Alexandria, Antioch, and Rome vie to be the most-important center, as greater heresy and persecution push the church underground. Persecution decreases as Christianity is accepted and promoted in the fourth paradigm. Constantinople struggles to overcome Antioch and Alexandria. The fifth, sixth, and seventh paradigms are rife with increased denominational feuds, greater corruption, and death. Roman emperor Justinian I adds Jerusalem and Constantinople to the three Christian centers, making a pentarchy, that results in the church's great schism of 1054. Despite the infighting, Christianity spreads quickly due to early ninth- to end of the thirteenth-century crusades.

Increased church corruption in the late Middle Ages, the fourteenth and fifteenth centuries, results in the rise of Christian reformers. In the sixteenth and seventeenth centuries, intellect overcomes might as scientific and biblical knowledge is pursued. During the eighth paradigm the printing press makes the Bible the book for all people. The ninth paradigm brings problems and blessings as dark sides of economic, industrial progress, in addition to an explosion of knowledge, bring enlightenment and evil that forever haunt church and state. In the tenth paradigm, humans believe life is happier outside of God's will. Slavery is abolished. Dissonance over governing styles motivates people to vie for what is best for them. A skewed sense of freedom in the twentieth century ushers in the eleventh paradigm, setting the stage for the twenty-first century's post-Christian world. In the twelfth paradigm, many believe that individual pleasure and happiness is achieved with everyone self-determining their lives. Power struggles hide agendas as corruption and hatred blossom, aligning and dividing along complex lines. At best, God is doubted, as lawlessness, lovelessness, and godlessness increase.

APPENDIX II
The Ten Commandments
and the Lord's Prayer

And God spoke all these words, saying,

"I am the LORD your God, who brought you out of the land of Egypt, out of the house of slavery. You shall have no other gods before me.

You shall not make for yourself a carved image, or any likeness of anything that is in heaven above, or that is in the earth beneath, or that is in the water under the earth. You shall not bow down or serve them, for I the LORD your God am a jealous God, visiting the iniquity of the fathers on the children to the third or fourth generation of those who hate Me, but showing steadfast love to thousands of those who love Me and keep My commandments.

You shall not take the name of the LORD your God in vain, for the LORD will not hold him guiltless who takes His name in vain.

Remember the Sabbath day, to keep it Holy. Six days you shall labor, and do all your work, but the seventh day is the Sabbath to the LORD your God. On it you shall not do any work, you, or your son, or your daughter, your male servant, or your female servant, or your livestock, or the sojourner who is within your gates. For in six days the LORD made heaven and earth, the sea, and all that is in them, and rested on the seventh day. Therefore the LORD blessed the Sabbath day and made it holy.

Honor your father and your mother, that your days may be long in the land that the LORD your God is giving you.

You shall not murder.

You shall not commit adultery.

You shall not steal.

You shall not bear false witness against your neighbor.

You shall not covet your neighbor's house; you shall not covet your neighbor's wife, or his male servant, or his female servant, or his ox, or his donkey, or anything that is your neighbor's." (Exod. 20:1–17)

The Ten Commandments, foundational to much of the world, remain a part of Judaism and Christianity. To understand why Jesus told John to write letters to seven churches of Revelation, we must know the commandments God gave to Moses for Israel. They were taught and followed in the early church but over time their importance has eroded.

The Bible reveals that the commandments were written with the finger of God on two tablets of stone that Moses cut (Exod. 31:18; 32:15–16). Before this, Moses wrote down the commandments and laws that God had commanded him to do (Exod. 24:4). Under Mosaic law, after a trial Levite priests were responsible for enforcing the death penalty for crimes that had broken some of the commandments, including worshipping other gods, blasphemy, breaking the Sabbath, dishonoring parents, and adultery.

The first four commandments teach how Christians must honor and serve God; the last six are about how Christians are to treat others. Regarding the Sabbath and Christians, Exodus 31:12,16 states that the Sabbath (last day of the week) is for the Israelites. Christians hold the first day, the Lord's Day, as sacred. Some Christians hold Saturday and Sunday, the last and first days of the week, as days for God and family.

Jesus's instructions to the church went beyond Israel's commandments and 613 laws. Jesus said that He came to fulfill the law, not to abolish it (Matt. 5:17–20). He taught that Christians must love their enemies (Matt. 5:43–48). Even being angry with a brother for no cause was the same as breaking the law (Matt. 5:21–22, 44). Jesus said that coveting or thinking of sinning is the same as committing it (Matt. 5:27–28).

The old Jewish covenant is a ministry of death, as it does not lead to repentance and change. Christ's death, the New Covenant, leads to God's Spirit putting His laws in minds and writing them on hearts so that Christians want to obey them (Heb. 8:10).

One of Jesus's most-famous teachings and one which many new Christians want to learn and use is the "Our Father," or the "Lord's Prayer," of Matthew 6:5–15.[120]

> Our Father in heaven, hallowed be Your name. Your kingdom come, Your will be done, on earth as it is in heaven. Give us this day our daily bread, and forgive us our debts, as we also have forgiven our debtors. And lead us not into temptation, but deliver us from evil, for yours is the kingdom, the power, and the glory forever and ever. Amen. (Matt. 6:9b–13)

Christians desire to know God and understand His Word better, knowing that they will never achieve perfection. They know that they must read the Bible, guard it with their hearts, cover reading and study in prayer, while being extremely careful how they interpret it. Confusion over meaning is human generated, not of God. Idolizing specific preachers, writers, and/or doctrine can block or hamper understanding. Also, the devil's interference must never be downplayed.

Christians must have faith in God and the Bible as God's Word to understand its meaning for life. God will ensure that enough is understood to guarantee salvation and that His will is achieved. Christians must be humble enough to accept that they cannot know everything, but that they know and love He who does.

---

[120] *ESV Study Bible* (2008), 1832. "For yours is the kingdom, the power, and the glory, forever. Amen" is perhaps a later addition, as it is not in the oldest Greek manuscripts. Based on 1 Chronicles 29:11–13, these words are theologically sound and appropriate for use in worship.

APPENDIX III

Chiastic Structure of the Letters to the Seven Churches

A To Ephesus (Rev. 2:1-7)—juxtaposed to Philadelphia, B¹ (**GREATEST LOVE LOST**—*CHURCH INSTITUTED*—Harbor silted up)

   B To Smyrna (Rev. 2:8-11)—juxtaposed to Laodicea, A¹ (**FAITHFUL ENDURANCE**—*POOR but SENSING*—Living Water)

      C To Pergamum (Rev. 2:12-17) (*FIGHTING GOD*—**TOLERATING SIN**—of the devil)

         D To Thyatira (Rev. 2:18-29) (*FIGHTING GOD*—**ACCEPTING SIN**—of the flesh)

      C¹ To Sardis (Rev. 3:1-6) (*FIGHTING GOD*—**PROMOTING SIN**—of the world)

   B¹ To Philadelphia (Rev. 3:7-13)—juxtaposed to Ephesus, A (**FAITHFUL LOVE**— AWAKE and READY—Bread of Life)

A¹ To Laodicea (Rev. 3:14-22)—juxtaposed to Smyrna, B (**HOPELESSLY LOST**—*RICH but SENSELESS*—Useless Water)

The two As had serious water issues. They reflect the beginning and the end of the church on earth: A is Ephesus, some say founded by Paul, and therefore may be the only one of the seven not founded by John, although he spent many years there and probably died there. It represents the beginning of the church's initial organization and development into institutions. What began as Christ's Body founded on truth in God's love quickly eroded, as humans took the helm. God's love and truth were overridden by human and worldly power. Ephesus held to the truth but lost its heart. It is juxtaposed to B¹, Philadelphia, who loves and is loved by God. Not loving God breaks the first commandment, jeopardizing salvation.

Opposite Ephesus is Laodicea, A¹, which represents the church in spiritual battle before Jesus's second coming. These are like two sides of a coin, but A¹, Laodicea, is worse: no love and no truth. Laodicea neither sees nor hears. It is self-sufficient, with no need of God. Its church serves no purpose. It is so bad that Jesus wants to spit it out of His mouth. It is hopeless. Revival is unlikely, if not impossible. This church should sound the alarm to churches today. Those in churches serving no purpose but simply going through the motions must be attentive to Jesus's revelation. Both A, Ephesus, and A¹, Laodicea, contrast to B, Smyrna, and B¹, Philadelphia, the two faithful churches.

B, Smyrna, and B¹, Philadelphia, are the conquerors, the overcomers, which Jesus did not rebuke. They reflect the true church: the saved, the redeemed, those whose robes are white, who will receive the crown, the tree of life, and be pillars in God's temple. No consequences are imposed for disobedience because they are obedient. These two churches represent the persecution that the church has endured, is enduring, and will continue to endure. Smyrna and Philadelphia lived the agape love of God. They exhibited God's truth in love to all they encountered, as they drank freely of the living water and ate fully of the spiritual bread. Both churches faithfully and patiently endure until Jesus returns, modeling what faith means to Christians and the world. These two churches illuminate the Word of God.

The two Cs and the D represent three ways that humans are tempted to sin. C, Pergamum, and C¹, Sardis, reflect sin that happens whenever one capitulates to temptation outside the self: sin of the devil and sin of the world. Pergamum denotes the spiritual war that has gone on from the beginning—the devil uses every weapon in his arsenal to fight God, His Son, the Holy Spirit, and the Bible. Many in the Pergamum church succumbed to the devil, but God's sharp two-edged sword that cuts to soul and spirit is victorious. Most in the Sardis church were defeated by the devil's scheme that promoted all forms of worship to be of the world, assimilate into society, and be good, happy people. The church in Thyatira, D, represents the carnal church. It describes people's individual, innate struggles against the sinful desires of their own flesh. The flesh, the world, and the devil tempt Christians to sin and fall from grace which, if not repented of, impacts their eternal security. The letters to these three churches represent sin's progression from toleration and acceptance to promotion of it.

Printed in the United States
by Baker & Taylor Publisher Services

Printed in the United States
by Baker & Taylor Publisher Services